MEETING JESUS IN THE GOSPELS

MEETING
JESUS
IN THE
GOSPELS

GEORGE
MARTIN

PUBLISHED BY ST. ANTHONY MESSENGER PRESS
CINCINNATI, OHIO

These reflections appeared in *New Covenant*, except for "What Did Jesus Look Like?" which appeared in *Catholic Digest*. Many of these reflections were also published in *God's Word: Reading Scripture with George Martin* (Our Sunday Visitor Books, 1998). All have been revised for this book.

Scripture selections are taken from the *New Revised Standard Version of the Bible*, Copyright © 1989 by the Division of Christian Education of the National Council of the Churches of Christ in the United States of America, and used by permission. All rights reserved.

Note: The editors of this volume have made minor changes in capitalization to some of the Scripture quotations herein. Please consult the original source for proper capitalization.

Unless otherwise noted, quotations from Vatican II documents are from Austin Flannery, ed., *Vatican Council II, Volume 1: The Conciliar and Post Conciliar Documents*, rev. ed. (Northport, N.Y.: Costello, 1998).

Cover design by Candle Light Studios
Book design by Jennifer Tibbits
Cover image © Digital Stock

LIBRARY OF CONGRESS CATALOGING-IN-PUBLICATION DATA

Martin, George, 1939-
Meeting Jesus in the Gospels / George Martin.
p. cm.
Includes bibliographical references (p.   ) and index.
ISBN 978-0-86716-900-3 (pbk. : alk. paper) 1. Jesus Christ—Meditations. 2. Bible. N.T. Gospels—Meditations. 3. Catholic Church—Prayers and devotions. I. Title.
BS2555.54.M27 2009
232.9—dc22

2008049297

ISBN 978-0-86716-900-3

Published by Servant Books, an imprint of St. Anthony Messenger Press
28 W. Liberty St.
Cincinnati, OH 45202
www.ServantBooks.org

Printed in the United States of America.

Printed on acid-free paper.

09 10 11 12 13 5 4 3 2 1

FOR JIM & SUSAN MANNEY

CONTENTS

PREFACE

We would like to meet Jesus.

We would like to have walked with him along the shore of the Sea of Galilee, listening to his words, experiencing his love. We envy those who did, whom he called his friends (John 15:15). And we look forward to being with him in eternity, when we will "see his face" (Revelation 22:4) and experience the fullness of his love. But even now, here on earth in the twenty-first century, we yearn to know him better.

The Gospels are a privileged place for meeting Jesus. As the bishops gathered in the Second Vatican Council proclaimed, "Among all the inspired writings, even among those of the New Testament, the Gospels have a special place, and rightly so, because they are our principal source for the life and teaching of the Incarnate Word, our Savior" (*Dei Verbum*, 18). The bishops also proclaimed, quoting Saint Jerome, that "ignorance of the Scriptures is ignorance of Christ" (*Dei Verbum,* 25). So we must read and reread the four Gospels, pondering what they tell us about Jesus, listening to his words, observing his actions.

We must also ponder what Jesus tells us about how we are to live as his friends and disciples. We do not meet Jesus as one might meet a celebrity, hoping to be photographed with him so that we can hang the photo on a wall to impress our friends. We meet Jesus to receive life from him and to become like him. We learn his teachings so that we may live by them. We do not read about the first disciples because they are interesting people but so that we can profit from their example of what we should do—and not do—as followers of Jesus. Our reflections on the Gospels cannot be detached analysis. We read the Gospels to be transformed by the one whom we read about, to enter into the mystery of his life in the hope of sharing his life eternally.

The reflections in this book were written over the course of several decades as the fruit of my meditations on the Gospels. They crisscross the Gospels, sometimes returning to the same passages for different considerations. They are, as it were, snapshots of Jesus, sometimes several of the same scene taken from different angles.

The best way to meet Jesus in the Gospels is by following the church's traditional method of reading the Scriptures—*lectio divina,* Latin for "sacred reading." In its simplest form *lectio divina* involves reading, reflecting and praying: Reading a portion of Scripture, reflecting on its meaning and its implications for oneself and then responding in prayer. I have included questions to help stimulate your reflections, so that as you read the Gospels you may meet and speak with Jesus.

George Martin
Lent 2008

ONE

GETTING TO KNOW JESUS

Who do you say that I am?

MARK 8:29

WHAT DID JESUS LOOK LIKE?

Is not this the carpenter…?

MARK 6:3

The Gospels do not describe what Jesus looked like. They proclaim him to be the Son of God and Messiah, and that he is, regardless of whether he was tall or short, long-haired or bald. Artists have portrayed him in different ways through the centuries—most often looking like the people of their own culture.

We can surmise, though, that Jesus looked like the people of his culture: He was to all appearances a first-century Galilean Jew. Some of his neighbors in Nazareth found him so ordinary in appearance—so much like them, in other words—that they could not accept the fact that he was anything more than a first-century Jew.

3

How did first-century Galilean Jews look? They were on the average shorter than people are today. A study of Galilean burial remains shows that the average adult man was five foot five, and the average woman, four foot ten. Some Galilean Jew features have probably been handed down to Middle Eastern Jews of today. But since body build and facial features differ even within ethnic groups, this doesn't tell us much about Jesus as an individual.

The Gospels do, however, give us some important clues about the general physical condition of Jesus. The first clue is that Jesus was a carpenter. Immediately images of carpenters come to our minds—perhaps shirtless young men framing a house on a hot summer day. But is this the kind of carpenter Jesus was?

The Gospels use the Greek word *tekton* to describe the occupation of Jesus and Joseph, a word Bibles translate as "carpenter." But a *tekton* was one who worked with any hard and lasting material, including stone as well as wood. Houses in Nazareth usually had stone walls; wood was used sparingly for roof beams, doors and door frames. Did Jesus work with stone as well as wood? He probably did. Archaeologists estimate the population of Nazareth at the time of Jesus to be only a few hundred people. How many woodworkers and stonemasons did such a village need? Perhaps Joseph & Son served most of the construction and handyman needs of Nazareth, from building a house wall to repairing a chair.

There were, obviously, no power tools in the time of Jesus. Wooden planks and stone blocks had to be cut and shaped with hand tools. Since trades were passed from father to son, Jesus would have grown up helping Joseph hew beams and wrestle foundation stones into place—everything that a village *tekton* was called upon to do. I visited an archaeological dig in Israel, excavating first-century Bethsaida. A group of young, muscular workmen were moving a stone from the wall of a house, and it took all their strength. As a *tekton*, Jesus probably strained with similar stones.

When Jesus spoke of a house built on rock that could withstand winds and floods better than a house built on sand (Matthew 7:24–27), he spoke as one who had laid his share of foundations. When he quoted Psalm 118's reference to a stone rejected by builders that became a cornerstone (Psalm 118:22; Mark 12:10), he echoed his own experience in sorting building blocks and choosing cornerstones.

I therefore think that Jesus was a rather rugged man, with heavily callused hands and well-developed muscles. I don't know whether he was stocky or lanky, but he was strong. He could put in a full day of hard manual work, day after day.

When I was in college, I applied for a shovel job on a pipeline crew. The foreman looked at my uncallused hands and shook his head; it was obvious that I was not used to such work. After some pleas I got the job anyway, and a good many blisters that summer. Had it been Jesus applying for the job, the foreman would have taken one look at his hands and hired him on the spot. I doubt Jesus would have developed any blisters.

I don't mean to imply that Jesus was a common laborer: A *tekton* was a skilled occupation, requiring the mastery of a variety of tools and materials. Jesus could have crafted a better table or chest than I could ever hope to, even with power tools.

Another clue to the general physical condition of Jesus is found in what has been called "the fifth Gospel," the Holy Land. When we look at a map of the Holy Land, it can have the appearance of being flat. But as every pilgrim discovers, the Holy Land is very hilly. It is a steep climb up eighteen-hundred-foot-high Mount Tabor, the traditional site of Jesus' Transfiguration. It is a long upward journey from Capernaum to Caesarea Philippi in the foothills of Mount Hermon, the site of Peter's confession of faith. There is no level path from Galilee to Jerusalem; there are few level streets in Jerusalem itself.

For the ordinary person in the ancient world, travel was done on foot. Travelers would average fifteen to twenty miles a day, depending on the terrain. To go from Galilee to Jerusalem for pilgrimage feasts, which devout Jews did three times a year, would mean four to seven days of such walking, each way.

John's Gospel tells us that Jesus went to Jerusalem for major feasts. Hence our image of Jesus must be of a man who could walk seventy to eighty miles over the course of a few days to worship and teach in Jerusalem and then walk the same distance home—so that he could continue his ministry by walking from village to village in the hills of Galilee. Jesus said that he had "nowhere to lay his head" (Matthew 8:20): How many nights in the course of his travels did he sleep in a field, wrapped in his cloak? Jesus repeatedly went up hills to pray—a natural way of getting privacy for someone used to hiking steep terrain.

Jesus was in very good physical shape by modern American standards. He earned his living by the strength of his arms and back; he carried out his ministry on the strength of his legs.

Jesus said, "I am gentle and humble in heart" (Matthew 11:29). But we should not use this verse to form a mental image of Jesus as a soft, delicate person, someone who might have made his living by posing for holy cards. Rather, Jesus may have needed to reassure his listeners of his gentleness because he looked like a sturdy village *tekton.*

But gentle he was. Parents brought their infants to Jesus "that he might touch them" with his callused hands (Luke 18:15). Jesus wept at the death of his friend Lazarus, wept so profoundly that bystanders exclaimed, "See how he loved him!" (John 11:35–36).

Jesus' physical ruggedness should be kept in mind as we read the accounts of his passion and death. Matthew and Mark tell us that Pilate, the Roman governor, had Jesus scourged (Matthew 27:26; Mark 15:15). Roman scourges were generally leather thongs with pieces of bone or metal at their ends to tear through flesh and muscle. The Gospels do not tell us how severely Jesus was scourged, but they do tell us that soldiers later forced Simon of Cyrene to carry Jesus' cross.

What was normally carried was not the entire cross but the crossbeam; the upright portion of a cross was a post permanently implanted at a place of execution. The crossbeam would be laid across the shoulders of a condemned man and so carried to the place of crucifixion. But according to Matthew, Mark and Luke, Jesus needed help carrying the crossbeam, and Simon was made to carry it instead of him. As a carpenter Jesus had undoubtedly carried many beams in his life, some for sizable distances and some of them far heavier than this crossbeam. But he was now incapable of bearing its load; that is an index of how horribly his muscles had been torn by scourging.

God could have chosen to send his Son to be the adopted son of someone with a desk job—a scribe or perhaps even a tax collector—so that Jesus would assume that occupation. But in God's plan Jesus was a *tekton* with a body hardened by work, and it was that body he gave up for us on the cross.

FOR REFLECTION

If I had been Jesus' next-door neighbor as he was growing up in Nazareth, what would have been my impression of him?

WHO IS JESUS?

*He asked his disciples, "Who do people say that
I am?" And they answered him, "John the
Baptist; and others, Elijah; and still others, one
of the prophets." He asked them, "But who do
you say that I am?" Peter answered him, "You
are the Messiah."*

MARK 8:27–29

In Jesus' quiz Peter had the right answer and others had wrong
answers, and we usually skip over the wrong answers rather
quickly. But even mistakes can teach lessons. Why did people
speculate that Jesus was Elijah or John the Baptist or one of the
prophets? What do their perceptions tell us about Jesus?

This was not the first time Jesus was identified with other
figures. Herod Antipas had heard about Jesus, "and he was per-
plexed, because it was said by some that John had been raised
from the dead, by some that Elijah had appeared, and by others
that one of the ancient prophets had arisen" (Luke 9:7–8). Jesus
was unique, and people did the only thing they could when
confronted with the unique: They tried to compare Jesus to
what they were familiar with. Jesus spoke in the name of God;
this made him like the prophets of old. But Jesus also worked
miracles and raised the dead, which the prophets didn't do,
except for Elijah and his successor Elisha (1 Kings 17:7–24; 2
Kings 4:18–37). So perhaps Jesus was another Elijah—maybe
even Elijah come back again (see Malachi 4:5–6).

If Jesus wasn't Elijah, then which prophet was he most like?
In Matthew's account of Peter's confession, Jeremiah is suggested (Matthew 16:14). Why Jeremiah? Perhaps because
Jeremiah warned that Jerusalem was heading for destruction,
and Jesus issued similar warnings (Luke 13:34–35; 19:41–44;

21:5–6, 20–24). Like Jeremiah, Jesus warned God's people what would happen if they continued on their present course.

Jesus also reminded some people of John the Baptist. In Matthew's Gospel, John announced that the kingdom of God was at hand and called people to repentance in preparation for its arrival (Matthew 3:1–2); Jesus proclaimed the same message (Matthew 4:17), making it natural for the two of them to be compared.

There were thus some elements of truth in the comparisons of Jesus to Elijah, to Jeremiah and to John the Baptist. Elijah performed wonders and raised the dead, and so did Jesus. Jeremiah warned that Jerusalem was on the road to disaster, and so did Jesus. John the Baptist announced that God was going to act soon to establish his reign on earth, and so did Jesus. But you would have to roll all of these figures into one to even begin to do justice to Jesus.

Jesus not only announced that the reign of God was at hand; he said that God was establishing his reign through him. His healing and exorcisms were part of the coming of God's kingdom (Luke 11:20).

Peter did better than others in perceiving Jesus' identity: Jesus was not like anyone of the past, not even the greatest of the past rolled together. Jesus was the Messiah, the agent God was using to establish his reign on earth. Peter didn't understand the full character of Jesus' messiahship, particularly that Jesus was a messiah who would suffer and die (Mark 8:31–33). But God graced Peter to perceive that Jesus was far more significant than was commonly supposed: Jesus was the Messiah.

We no less than Jesus' first followers have to struggle to comprehend his identity. As fully human and fully divine, Jesus Christ is unique in a way that our minds can never fathom. We too have to rely on limited insights for the light they shed on

Jesus. He is our friend and Savior, he is our brother and our Lord, he is Son of God and Word made flesh. But he is also infinitely more than words can express—as we will vividly realize when we see him face-to-face in eternity.

FOR REFLECTION

Who do I say Jesus is? How does my life show who Jesus is?

GOOD NEWS

The beginning of the good news of Jesus Christ, the Son of God....

Now after John was arrested, Jesus came to Galilee, proclaiming the good news of God, and saying, "The time is fulfilled, and the kingdom of God has come near; repent, and believe in the good news."

MARK 1:1, 14–15

The English word *gospel* comes from the Anglo-Saxon *godspell*, which means "good news." This is a literal translation of the Greek word *evangelion*, used by Mark to describe his book and to tell us that Jesus came to Galilee proclaiming good news and inviting people to believe in this good news.

Mark did not invent the word *evangelion*: It is found in ancient Greek literature as a technical term for a message of victory or other message that brought joy. Mark (and earlier Paul) adopted this word to describe the message of Jesus. It was an apt term.

God was doing something new in Jesus Christ, so a report on it was newsworthy. God was doing something very good for us through Jesus, so the report was not only news but good news. It was a message of victory, Jesus' victory over sin and death; it was a message that should bring joy to everyone who heard it. On every count it was appropriate for Mark to begin his book with the words, "The beginning of the good news of Jesus Christ." It was so appropriate that his book would eventually be called *good news*—or a *gospel*.

Jesus' first words in the Gospel of Mark are likewise concerned with good news: "The time is fulfilled, and the kingdom of God has come near; repent, and believe in the good news." The good news Jesus brought was that the moment had arrived for the reign of God to be established. For long centuries sin and suffering and death had reigned over the earth. Now God was acting through Jesus to conquer sin and suffering and death. God's reign was becoming present in the person of Jesus, through his teachings and healings and exorcisms: "If it is by the Spirit of God that I cast out demons, then the kingdom of God has come to you" (Matthew 12:28). That's good news! That's a message of victory that should bring us joy.

Yet two thousand years later, there is still sin and suffering and death. The reign of God has begun among us, but it has not yet reached its fulfillment. Jesus taught that he would return in power to establish the definitive reign of God. He asked us to pray for this to happen, for that is really what we are asking for when we pray the prayer that Jesus taught us: "Father in heaven, glorify your name, establish your reign, carry out your will." Jesus assured us that our prayers would be heard (Matthew 6:7–10; Luke 11:2–13). This is good news for us: Jesus will complete his work, so there is hope for the world and hope for us.

Do we fully accept this good news, this message of Jesus' victory? Or has this news grown stale in our ears? Has it lost its element of being good news for us, and does it no longer bring us joy? Perhaps we need to adjust our thinking. Jesus' invitation, "Repent and believe in the good news," could be translated, "Change your mind and believe in the good news." The Greek word for repentance *(metanoia)* literally means "a change of mind." Changed behavior should result from a change of mind, but true repentance begins in the mind and heart.

Jesus' invitation could be paraphrased: Change your thinking and accept the fact that the gospel message is really good news. Change the way you look at this world; perceive the signs of God's reign. Change your expectations for what lies ahead, and live in hope. Believe what I tell you, for it is the best possible news for you.

FOR REFLECTION
What is my response to the good news Jesus brings? Do I embrace it as good news for me?

JESUS' PRAYER

> *He was praying in a certain place, and after he*
> *had finished, one of his disciples said to him,*
> *"Lord, teach us to pray…."*

LUKE 11:1

The Gospels describe Jesus spending a lot of time in prayer. "Many crowds would gather to hear him and to be cured of their diseases. But he would withdraw to deserted places and pray" (Luke 5:15–16). "In the morning, while it was still very dark, he got up and went out to a deserted place, and there he prayed" (Mark 1:35). Jesus' ministry of proclaiming the kingdom of God and healing the afflicted was important, but prayer was essential, even at the cost of sleep.

On one occasion Jesus "withdrew from there in a boat to a deserted place by himself" (Matthew 14:13) to pray but was thwarted by crowds who followed him. After healing and feeding them, Jesus tried again, sending the disciples off in a boat. He "went up the mountain by himself to pray" and prayed until "early in the morning" (Matthew 14:23, 25)—literally, until the fourth watch of the night, which ran from 3:00 to 6:00 AM. Jesus spent most of the night in prayer.

Jesus rose very early or stayed up very late to pray, even spending whole nights in prayer (Luke 6:12). The disciples apparently got used to this, which might account for their behavior on several occasions. When Jesus "went up on the mountain to pray" and was transfigured, Peter, James and John became drowsy (Luke 9:28–32). Later Jesus went to Gethsemane to pray, and these disciples fell asleep (Mark 14:32–42). One Scripture scholar suggests that the disciples probably thought, "He's at it again. Another all-nighter—we might as well catch a few winks."

Yet Jesus' followers were so impressed with his prayer life that they wanted to be able to pray as he prayed. "Lord," they asked him, "teach us to pray." In response Jesus taught them the Our Father (Luke 11:1–4).

It is striking that the prayer that Jesus taught his followers is a short prayer—one of the shortest prayers in the Bible. Of the 150 psalms, only about five are as short as the Our Father. It was not accidental that Jesus taught his followers a short prayer, for he told them, "When you are praying, do not heap up empty phrases as the Gentiles do; for they think that they will be heard because of their many words. Do not be like them" (Matthew 6:7–8).

What a paradox! Jesus spent whole nights in prayer but told his followers that long prayers were unnecessary, and he taught them a prayer that they could recite in twenty seconds. What's going on here?

One answer seems to be that what is important is not so much the words we use in our prayers, and certainly not the quantity of words, but rather the attitude with which we pray. Jesus taught his followers to pray to his Father as their Father. There is good evidence that Jesus taught his followers to call upon God as *Abba*, just as he did (Mark 14:36). When Paul wrote to Greek-speaking Gentile Christians in Rome and Galatia, he reminded them that they used the Aramaic word *Abba* when they prayed (Romans 8:15; Galatians 4:6).

Abba is the informal word children used to address their father, perhaps best translated as "Dad." God as our *Abba* is not a distant and reserved Father but a close and loving Father. Our *Abba* in heaven is a Father we can turn to with complete trust and confidence. Thus we do not need to multiply words when we pray—"your Father knows what you need before you ask him" (Matthew 6:8).

That is why Jesus could spend a whole night in prayer and not need to use many words: He was in communion with his *Abba*. And that is why we do not need to ramble on endlessly when we pray. We do not need to change the mind of an aloof and uncaring God. We need only acknowledge that God is indeed our Father and loves us; we need only express our trust in him; we need only enter into communion with our *Abba*.

FOR REFLECTION

How might I better imitate Jesus' example of praying to his Father?

JESUS READ SCRIPTURE

*About the middle of the festival Jesus went up
into the temple and began to teach. The Jews
were astonished at it, saying, "How does this
man have such learning, when he has never
been taught?"*

JOHN 7:14–15

Scholars were a specialized profession in ancient times. They were men who knew how to read and write; hence one title for them was "scribe." They had studied under an older scholar as their master and in turn taught others; another title scholars therefore bore was "teacher."

Being a scholar was normally a full-time profession requiring long preparation. The book of Sirach describes various ordinary occupations, such as farmer, blacksmith and potter, and then contrasts the scribe to them. Only those with the leisure to study could become scholars:

> *The wisdom of the scribe depends on the opportunity of
>   leisure;*
> *only the one who has little business can become wise.*
> *How can one become wise who handles the plow,*
> *...*
> *who drives oxen and is occupied with their work...?*
> *...*
> *How different the one who devotes himself*
>   *to the study of the law of the Most High! (Sirach*
>   *38:24–25, 34)*

This specialization of occupations helps us understand the amazement of the people of Nazareth when Jesus began his public ministry. "On the sabbath he began to teach in the synagogue, and many who heard him were astounded. They said, 'Where did this man get all this? What is this wisdom that has been given to him?… Is not this the carpenter?' " (Mark 6:2–3). The people of Nazareth were surprised that this Jesus who had been doing their carpentry work should suddenly begin acting like a teacher.

Jesus' background was a source of surprise in Jerusalem as well. When he began to teach in the temple precincts, the Jews wondered, "How does this man have such learning?"—literally, how does this man know letters, meaning, how is he able to read the Scriptures? They observed that Jesus had "never been taught," meaning that he had not studied under someone. They were amazed that Jesus knew the Scriptures so well without having been trained as a scholar.

We are probably less surprised by Jesus' knowledge of Scripture. After all, we might think, Jesus was divine: He knew everything. But this overlooks his full humanity. Because he fully shared our human condition, Jesus had to learn by the same slow, painful process by which we learn (see Luke 2:40, 52). He had to read through the books of the Old Testament, scroll by scroll, in order to grasp their meaning. As fully divine, Jesus was completely receptive to the graces of the Spirit, which enlightened his reading. But his knowledge of Scripture began with his own careful reading of the inspired texts.

Jesus was thoroughly immersed in the words and meaning of Scripture, and it was in light of Scripture that he understood his own mission. His first sermon in Nazareth was a proclamation that he fulfilled a prophecy of Isaiah (Luke 4:16–21). He told his followers that he would be put to death in fulfillment of the Scriptures (Luke 18:31–33). He criticized those who rejected him because they failed to understand the Scriptures and what they said about him (John 5:39–40, 46–47). And after his Resurrection he opened the eyes of his followers to understand what he had been trying to teach them all along: that he was the fulfillment of Scripture (Luke 24:25–27, 44–48).

Jesus was not a Scripture scholar by profession but someone who read and pondered the Word of God and understood his own life in light of that Word. In this Jesus is an example for those of us who are not professional scholars but bricklayers and homemakers, nurses and salespeople. There is certainly a place for scholars: Sirach's words in praise of them are, after all, a part of inspired Scripture. But everyone who follows Jesus, scholar or not, is addressed by the Word of God. Each of us should treasure the Scriptures no less than Jesus did; each of us should study them as Jesus studied them; each of us should understand the meaning of our lives in light of Scripture, as did Jesus.

FOR REFLECTION

On average, how much time each week do I devote to reading Scripture? How might I better imitate Jesus' example of reading and pondering Scripture?

THE SMALL WORLD OF JESUS

Then he began to reproach the cities in which most of his deeds of power had been done, because they did not repent. "Woe to you, Chorazin! Woe to you, Bethsaida! For if the deeds of power done in you had been done in Tyre and Sidon, they would have repented long ago…. And you, Capernaum,… if the deeds of power done in you had been done in Sodom, it would have remained until this day."

MATTHEW 11:20–21, 23

Jesus used Capernaum as his base of operations during his pubic ministry. He "made his home in Capernaum" (Matthew 4:13; see also Mark 2:1); it was "his own town" (Mathew 9:1). Jesus apparently lived in Peter's house (Mark 1:29–33). Archaeologists have uncovered the remains of this house; it is a roughly twenty-by-twenty-foot room, sharing a courtyard with similar one-room dwellings.

Except for traveling to Jerusalem, the Gospels do not describe Jesus venturing too far from Capernaum, at least by modern standards of travel. Tyre (Mark 7:24) was thirty-six miles from Capernaum; Caesarea Philippi (Matthew 16:13), twenty-seven miles. All the other sites in and around Galilee mentioned in the Gospels were closer, within a day's walk.

Even within this limited world, Jesus spent a good deal of time in Capernaum, Chorazin and Bethsaida, judging from his profound disappointment at the lack of response he received in these towns. Chorazin was two miles north of Capernaum; Bethsaida was four miles northeast of Capernaum and three miles from Chorazin. According to Matthew, it was in this small region that Jesus worked "most of his deeds of power," his healings and exorcisms.

These were not large towns. Archaeologists estimate that Capernaum had a population of between six hundred and fifteen hundred people, and that Chorazin and Bethsaida had populations of only several hundred each. A cluster of fishing and farming villages about three miles apart, less than an hour's walk from each other—that is a small world indeed! Yet Jesus chose to focus his efforts on the people of this small world.

We can ponder why Jesus made this choice. He certainly could have done otherwise: Larger cities would have given him potentially larger audiences. Perhaps there was an essentially personal character to Jesus' mission; perhaps it had to be carried out one-on-one, face-to-face, and could not be accomplished simply by addressing large crowds.

This gives us a glimpse of the particularity of God's love. God is not content to love the human race as a whole; God loves each of us as individuals. God sent his Son Jesus to walk the paths of Galilee, share meals with the men and women of fishing and farming villages and enter tangibly into their lives. He through whom the universe came into being lived in a one-room house and spent his time with homemakers and children, fishermen and farmers. In Jesus, God humbled himself to our scale to express his love.

Capernaum, Chorazin and Bethsaida provide an additional index of God's humbling of himself out of love. By Jesus' evaluation, his mission to the people of these villages was a failure. It foreshadowed the rejection Jesus would meet in Jerusalem, where his mission on earth would end in the failure of the cross. Jesus could have avoided the cross, just as he could have spared himself rejection by avoiding these three villages. But God's will for him was otherwise: Jesus had to bear God's love even to those who would spurn it. God is willing to fail in his love for us.

The Word becoming flesh and living among us is a great mystery; the way in which the incarnate Word lived among us heightens the mystery. Jesus did not behave like the emperor of Rome, a glorious figure on the world's stage. Jesus lived with and befriended ordinary people in small villages. Jesus gave his life to them—and ultimately gave his life for them. Jesus enters the world of our lives, however small it might be, however uneven our response to him.

FOR REFLECTION

What is the significance for me of Jesus' devoting so much of his time to the people of a few small villages? How has Jesus entered into my small world?

A DAY IN THE LIFE OF JESUS

The apostles gathered around Jesus, and told
him all that they had done and taught. He said
to them, "Come away to a deserted place all by
yourselves and rest a while." For many were
coming and going, and they had no leisure even
to eat. And they went away in the boat to a
deserted place by themselves. Now many saw
them going and recognized them, and they hur-
ried there on foot from all the towns and arrived
ahead of them. As he went ashore, he saw a
great crowd; and he had compassion for them....

MARK 6:30–34

Once Jesus emerged from his forty days in the wilderness, he was rarely alone again. There was usually a stream of people coming to him: blind beggars and bent women, leprous outcasts and argumentative lawyers, the demon-possessed and mentally impaired, the curious and the hostile, sinners and self-righteous, the diseased and the disturbed.

Jesus was incessantly besieged by people in need, whether on the road (Mark 10:46–52) or in the home of a friend. "When he returned to Capernaum after some days, it was reported that he was at home. So many gathered around that there was no longer room for them, not even in front of the door" (Mark 2:1–2). "Then he went home; and the crowd came together again, so that they could not even eat" (Mark 3:19–20).

Jesus could not enjoy a quiet evening by himself after a hard day's work. "That evening, at sundown, they brought to him all who were sick or possessed with demons. And the whole city was gathered around the door. And he cured many who were sick with various diseases, and cast out many demons" (Mark

1:32–34). Nor was he left in peace in the early morning hours. "In the morning, while it was still very dark, he got up and went out to a deserted place, and there he prayed. And Simon and his companions hunted for him. When they found him, they said to him, 'Everyone is searching for you' " (Mark 1:35–37).

It is never recorded that Jesus turned anyone away. No matter how tired he might have been, no matter who came to him, no matter how unreasonable their demands, Jesus responded with love. When he gazed on those who came to him, "he had compassion for them." The Greek word Mark uses for "compassion" means to be profoundly moved from one's inner depths; we might say that Jesus had a gut reaction of compassion.

Jesus expected his disciples to do the same. He commissioned them to perform the same works he performed (Mark 6:7–13), and he asked them to love as he loved (John 13:34–35; 15:12–17).

Jesus imposed no particular acts of penance on his followers; he did not ask them to fast, as did other spiritual leaders (see Mark 2:18). But inevitably the hardships of Jesus' life overflowed onto his disciples. The greatest hardship must have been the incessant crowds of those clamoring for help. If there was any particular penance in being a follower of Jesus, it was the penance of constant availability and lack of privacy. If there was any particular distinction to being known as a follower of Jesus, it was the distinction of being expected to do what he did.

When Jesus, Peter, James and John came down from the Mount of Transfiguration and rejoined the rest of the disciples, "they saw a great crowd around them" (Mark 9:14) who were seeking healing from the disciples as they sought healing from Jesus. A man told Jesus that his son was afflicted by a spirit that made him unable to speak and that "I asked your disciples to cast it out" (Mark 9:17–18).

It is not easy to be expected to do the same things as Jesus. It is not easy to become known as someone who helps others, for to the extent we are really helpful, many more may come to us in need. It is not easy to have our time taken over by those who are hurting or hungry or thirsting for a message of hope.

Neither was it easy for Jesus. But he didn't complain: He was about his Father's work, as he invites us to be (John 5:17; 20:21).

FOR REFLECTION

How do I respond when demands are placed on me? What does Jesus' example mean for me when I feel overwhelmed by demands?

JOHN'S QUESTION

When John heard in prison what the Messiah was doing, he sent word by his disciples and said to him, "Are you the one who is to come, or are we to wait for another?" Jesus answered them, "Go and tell John what you hear and see: the blind receive their sight, the lame walk, the lepers are cleansed, the deaf hear, the dead are raised, and the poor have good news brought to them. And blessed is anyone who take no offense at me."

MATTHEW 11:2–6

At first reading, both John the Baptist's question and Jesus' reply are puzzling. Why should John ask whether Jesus was the one who was to come: Had not John already proclaimed Jesus to be the more powerful one who would come after him and baptize with the Holy Spirit and fire (Matthew 3:11)? And in responding, why would Jesus list the works he was doing, since John already knew about these works (Matthew 11:2)? And why would Jesus be worried about being the source of scandal?

John had indeed announced the coming of one more powerful than himself, one who would bring the Holy Spirit, and John had recognized Jesus as this person (see Matthew 3:14). But it also seems that John expected this person to execute God's judgment upon the world:

> *Even now the ax is lying at the root of the trees; every tree therefore that does not bear good fruit is cut down and thrown into the fire.... His winnowing fork is in his hand, and he will clear his threshing floor and will gather his wheat into the granary; but the chaff he will burn with unquenchable fire. (Matthew 3:10, 12)*

Jesus didn't act as John expected him to act. Jesus passed up opportunities to condemn sinners (see John 8:10–11) and instead created opportunities to be with them (Luke 19:1–10). Jesus' association with sinners scandalized the Pharisees (Matthew 9:10–11) and may have scandalized John the Baptist as well—or at least disappointed him. Rather than wielding an ax or burning chaff in fire, Jesus fulfilled Isaiah's prophecy, "He will not break a bruised reed / or quench a smoldering wick" (Isaiah 42:1–4; Matthew 12:17–21).

Jesus in his answer to John the Baptist repeated what John already knew but described his actions in terms that echoed prophecies of Isaiah (Isaiah 29:18–19; 35:5–6; 61:1–2). Jesus thereby implied that his coming was prophesied in the Old Testament. Jesus came as the servant of God, the one who would bear the sins of others rather than punish them for their sins (see Isaiah 52:13—53:12). He came not to condemn but to save (John 3:17).

Jesus did not live up to the expectations of others—not the Pharisees nor his disciples, who expected him to inaugurate an earthly kingdom (Acts 1:6), nor even John the Baptist. Hence Jesus said, "Blessed are those who are not scandalized by what I do. Happy is the one who believes in me for who I am and who my works reveal me to be."

But what then of John's prophecy of what Jesus would do? If Jesus did not go about separating the wheat from the chaff and burning the chaff, was John's prophecy false?

No, it was a true prophecy—but John did not understand the time of its fulfillment.

Jesus did speak of judgment but of judgment at the end of time (Matthew 25:31–46). His parable of the weeds sown in the field (Matthew 13:24–30) ends with these weeds' being burned, but the master forbids their being uprooted before the final harvest, lest the wheat also be harmed. The parable of the net thrown into the sea (Matthew 13:47–50) is also a parable of judgment but likewise judgment "at the end of the age" (Matthew 13:49). Not until then would John's prophecy be fulfilled. In the meantime the work of Jesus was to search out and save the lost (Luke 19:10). Jesus' urging of his followers to be cautious in passing judgment on others (Matthew 7:1–5) should be understood in this light.

If even John the Baptist could apparently be mistaken in his expectations of Jesus, how much more easily can we fail to understand him! The antidote must be to ponder the pages of the Gospels and meditate on how Jesus acted and what he taught.

That was what Jesus said in reply to John: Look at what I do, and listen to what I say. Don't make me conform to what you think I should be like, but look carefully and ponder what I am like. Happy are you who are not scandalized by my words and deeds but receive them as a revelation of my loving Father.

What about Jesus most puzzles me? Am I tripped up by any of his teachings or demands? Why do I find them difficult?

JESUS' POWERLESSNESS

He left that place and came to his home-
town... [and] began to teach..., and many
who heard him were astounded. They said,
"Where did this man get all this?... What
deeds of power are being done by his hands! Is
not this the carpenter, the son of Mary and
brother of James and Joses and Judas and
Simon, and are not his sisters here with us?"
And they took offense at him.... And he could
do no deed of power there, except that he laid
his hands on a few sick people and cured them.
And he was amazed at their unbelief.

MARK 6:1–3, 5–6

Why was Jesus unable to perform mighty deeds in his home-town of Nazareth? Matthew's Gospel states that it was because of the lack of faith he encountered: "And he did not do many deeds of power there, because of their unbelief" (Matthew 13:58). But this answer demands exploration.

Did the unbelief of the townspeople of Nazareth rob Jesus of his powers? Would he have been unable to turn water into wine in Nazareth, as he had done in Cana? This cannot be. Jesus was the Spirit-empowered Son of God (Luke 3:22; 4:14); his power was not a magical quality that switched off and on at the city limits. If we look only at Jesus' abilities, whatever he was capable of doing anywhere he was capable of doing in Nazareth. And in fact he did cure some sick people in Nazareth by laying his hands on them.

What then was the problem in Nazareth? I believe the key lies in the kind of "deeds of power" that Jesus performed. Nowhere do the Gospels describe Jesus performing a miracle except to meet some human need. He healed the sick, he freed the possessed, he saved his disciples from storms, he fed hungry crowds, he provided commercial fishermen with a good catch, and he even provided a coin for a necessary tax payment (Matthew 17:27). Yet despite his ability to perform mighty deeds, Jesus did not indulge in gratuitous displays of his power. He did not float down from the pinnacle of the temple (Matthew 4:5–7), he did not hurl mountains around like tennis balls (despite Matthew 17:20), he did not paint stripes on the moon. Jesus surely could have performed all sorts of spectaculars that would have awed the crowds, but he did not work wonders except to meet human needs.

We should also note that Jesus made no invariable demands on those he helped. He welcomed the faith of those who believed he had the ability to heal them, but he also healed those who demonstrated no faith, simply out of compassion for them—even those who did not ask to be healed (Luke 13:10–16), even those who did not know who he was (John 5:1–13).

What then happened in Nazareth? Jesus met with not only lack of faith but also positive disbelief. People took offense at who he claimed to be. The people of Nazareth were sure they knew who Jesus was, because he had grown up in their midst and had done carpentry work for them. Most of them rejected the possibility that he was anything other than a carpenter. The only kind of needs that they were willing to bring to Jesus might have been broken chairs and sagging doors.

The result was that Jesus did few mighty deeds in Nazareth, since he performed mighty deeds in response to human needs. He was quite capable of doing in Nazareth what he did elsewhere, but the people of Nazareth generally refused to bring their needs to him. Jesus found this refusal amazing. Even if he didn't demand faith as a condition for healing, he at least wanted more than positive rejection.

If this understanding of the incident at Nazareth is correct, then the only thing that prevents Jesus from helping us is our rejection of him, our refusal to come to him with our needs. Unbelief makes Jesus powerless in the sense that he can't do for us what we won't let him do. We should turn to Jesus with as much faith as we can muster but never hold back from him because we feel we do not have enough faith. Jesus simply wants the opportunity to help us.

For Reflection

What is my greatest need right now? How can I place it in Jesus' hands?

JESUS' AUNT

Standing near the cross of Jesus were his mother, and his mother's sister, Mary the wife of Clopas, and Mary Magdalene.

JOHN 19:25

Wasn't Mary an only child? We usually do not think of her having any brothers or sisters. They are not mentioned in the ancient writings that claim to provide details about the life of Mary not recorded in the Gospels. There is devotion to Mary's parents, Saints Joachim and Anne, but none, as far as I know, to any sister of Mary.

Yet there she is—Mary's sister—in John's Gospel, standing by the cross of Jesus along with Mary and two other Marys. She is not named by John; she is not Mary the wife of Clopas, because two sisters probably would not have both been named Mary.

Some speculate that the name of Mary's sister was Salome and that she was the wife of Zebedee and the mother of James and John, basing their speculation on a combination of Matthew 27:56 and Mark 15:40. This would make James and John cousins of Jesus and might explain why they thought they were due places of honor in Jesus' kingdom (Mark 10:35–37). But the evidence for such speculation is thin. The only certainty we have is that Mary did have a sister, and she was present at Jesus' crucifixion.

Since Mary's sister was Jesus' aunt, she very likely would have known Jesus as he was growing up. Perhaps she even lived near Joseph, Mary and Jesus in Nazareth: Extended families tended to cluster their dwellings around a shared courtyard with a baking oven. We can't know this, of course: The Gospels tell us nothing about Jesus' aunt and her interactions with Jesus through the years. Nor does Scripture say anything about her after Jesus' Resurrection. Acts tells us that the 120 disciples gathered in the Upper Room after Jesus' ascension included "certain women" along with Mary (Acts 1:13–15). Was Jesus' aunt one of them?

Another trick question: Was Paul an only child?

Paul never mentions having any brothers or sisters in his letters, nor did any make an appearance in Acts. But there is again a single verse to upset our preconceptions: "Now the son of Paul's sister heard about the ambush; so he went and gained entrance to the barracks and told Paul" (Acts 23:16). Paul had a sister who lived long enough to marry and bear a son. Perhaps she even outlived Paul; we have no way of knowing. We do not even know her name.

Do Jesus' aunt and Paul's sister have any lessons for us?

The silence of Scripture about the sisters of Mary and Paul is a reminder of the nature of Scripture. The Bible was not written to provide us with complete biographies of Jesus and of our ancestors in the faith. The purpose of Scripture is to teach "firmly, faithfully, and without error...that truth which God wanted put into the sacred writings for the sake of our salvation" (*Dei Verbum*, 11).[1] In providing us with saving truth, Scripture gives us glimpses of the lives of many people, above all Jesus. But the Bible does not aim at biographical completeness; it doesn't fill in all the blanks we might like to see filled in. The lives of these women are two of the blanks, and they remind us that that there are blanks in our knowledge of the life of Jesus as well.

These two women also bear a second message for us. Most Christians through the ages—most of those with whom we will share heaven—are anonymous. Most lived ordinary lives and were soon forgotten by all except their immediate descendants. Most of us will follow in their quickly forgotten footsteps.

These two largely forgotten women can serve as patron saints for all of the forgotten Christians through the ages and for us as well. We don't have to be famous to go to heaven or have extraordinary accomplishments that get written up in history books. We need to find salvation through Jesus, but that is all we need. Even if we are as quickly forgotten as were Jesus' aunt and the sister of Paul, we can still obtain the greatest prize that any human being can ever achieve: eternal life with God.

And once we are in heaven, these will be two interesting women to chat with!

FOR REFLECTION

What blanks in the Gospel accounts of the life of Jesus do I most wish had been filled in? Would my relationship with Jesus be any different if they were?

TWO

PONDERING
HIS LOVE

Jesus began to weep. So the Jews said, "See how he loved him!"

JOHN 11:35–36

JESUS' COMPASSION

As he went ashore, he saw a great crowd; and he had compassion for them, because they were like sheep without a shepherd; and he began to teach them many things.

MARK 6:34

In those days when there was again a great crowd without anything to eat, he called his disciples and said to them, "I have compassion for the crowd, because they have been with me now for three days and have nothing to eat."

MARK 8:1–2

The Gospel of Mark twice describes Jesus feeding a crowd of hungry people (Mark 6:30–44; 8:1–9). The first incident took place when Jesus tried to get away with his disciples for a needed rest, but people nevertheless tracked them down (Mark 6:31–34). Rather than be upset by the crowd's intrusion, Jesus had compassion on their spiritual needs and taught them, afterward feeding them as well. In the second incident Jesus was moved with compassion by the hunger of those who had been following him for three days, and he fed them.

Several things stand out in these two incidents. One is Jesus' instinctive reaction of compassion. He was not irritated that a crowd of people disrupted his quiet time; rather he was moved with compassion for them. He did not say to the crowds, "You should have had the foresight to pack a lunch"; he had compassion on them in their hunger.

Another lesson: Jesus is concerned about all our needs, physical as well as spiritual. He was moved with compassion by the empty stomachs of those who came to him as well as by their spiritual emptiness, and he fed them in both body and spirit.

In doing so Jesus was more than simply a kindly fellow wandering around the hills of Galilee. He is the image of the unseen God (Colossians 1:15); to gaze on him is to see his Father (John 14:9). Jesus' attitude toward us is therefore God's attitude toward us. In Jesus' compassion we are given a privileged glimpse of God's compassion.

That makes it worthwhile to reflect on the compassion Jesus had for the crowds. The Greek word Mark used to describe Jesus' compassion is vivid: *splangchnizomai*, a verb meaning "to have pity," comes from the noun *splangchna*, meaning "entrails" or "internal organs." The King James Version rendered this word as "bowels of compassion" (1 John 3:17, *KJV*). We might prefer to say "heartfelt mercy" or "compassion from the depths of one's being." Jesus did not have just a twinge of pity for those who came to him in need; he was profoundly moved with compassion for them, moved from his innermost being.

Jesus' spontaneous heartfelt compassion is an index of God's compassion for us. God is not mildly interested in our well-being; God is passionately concerned for us. He sent his Son as an expression of his compassion for us.

The word *compassion* itself gives us another clue to God's attitude toward us: *compassion* comes from the Latin for "suffer with." God demonstrated his compassion for us by sending his Son to be one of us and to take our suffering upon himself. In Jesus God suffers with us.

Suffering is a mystery. Why does a good God allow there to be so much suffering on this earth—particularly the suffering of innocent people caught up in wars and ravaged by famines, stricken by diseases and subject to untimely death? There is no glib answer to this question. There is, however, the image of Jesus on the cross. God has not abolished our suffering, but he has entered into it. God's compassion for us finds it ultimate and most vivid expression in his suffering with us in his Son.

FOR REFLECTION

What do I find most striking about the compassion of Jesus? If to see Jesus is to see the Father, what glimpse of God am I given in Jesus?

GOD'S COMPASSION

*The kingdom of heaven may be compared to a
king who wished to settle accounts with his
slaves. When he began the reckoning, one who*

owed him ten thousand talents was brought to him; and, as he could not pay, his lord ordered him to be sold, together with his wife and children and all his possessions, and payment to be made. So the slave fell on his knees before him, saying, "Have patience with me, and I will pay you everything." And out of pity for him, the lord of that slave released him and forgave him the debt.

MATTHEW 18:23–27

Just as Jesus' compassion is an expression of God's compassion, so God's compassion is an index of Jesus' compassion. One of Jesus' most vivid teachings about God's compassion is found in his parable about a slave who had been forgiven much but then refused to forgive a little (Matthew 18:23–35). This parable is a drama in several acts; we will consider just its first act, which has a lesson in itself.

The slave owed his master "ten thousand talents." "Ten thousand" was the largest number used in counting in Jesus' day; the best counterpart today might be a trillion. A "talent" was the largest monetary unit. Ten thousand talents would represent wages of around two hundred thousand years for an ordinary worker at the time of Jesus. The slave therefore owed a truly immense sum, far more than he could ever work off. His promise, "I will pay you everything," was ridiculous: It was impossible for him to repay what he owed.

But note what happened: "Out of pity for him, the lord of that slave released him and forgave him the debt." His master granted him complete forgiveness, giving him a fresh start.

That is probably not how you or I would have handled it. If someone owed us more money than they had, we might say,

"Pay what you can, even if you can't pay the full amount." Or, "Take some time to get your affairs in order, and then begin making payments." We would keep the debtor in debt to us so we could salvage as much as possible of what was owed us. Our least likely response would be, "I completely forgive your debt."

Yet the master of this slave made just this response—and Jesus' parable proclaims that this is what God is like. God extends forgiveness to those who owe him far more than they could ever repay. Moved with compassion, God wipes away our debts of sin, however great.

So goes Act One of this parable. Jesus presented this scene to prepare the way for the point of the parable: Since we have been forgiven by God, we should forgive others. No matter how much we may have to forgive, it will never come anywhere near matching the great amount that we have been forgiven. It is not that God has fixed a parking ticket for us, and now we have to forgive someone who has wrecked our new car. It's rather that God has forgiven us trillions, and we in turn need to pick up the lunch tab for others now and then.

The point of the whole parable should not be lost. But neither should the point of Act One. The reign of God begins with God's compassion toward us and his great forgiveness. God has first loved us; God has acted first to draw us to himself. We need to be concerned about the response we make to him, but we should never lose sight of the fact that it is a response—something we do because of what God has already done.

Most of us need a periodic reminder that our salvation begins with God: that he has acted first out of compassion for us, that he has loved us when we were not very lovable, that the magnitude of his compassionate love far overshadows anything we could ever do for him. John writes, "In this is love, not that we loved God but that he loved us and sent his Son to be the atoning sacrifice for our sins" (1 John 4:10). Jesus' mission and compassion is an expression of God's love and compassion for us—a truly immense compassion.

FOR REFLECTION

When have I experienced God's loving-kindness toward me? What little things might I do for others to imitate the compassion of Jesus?

MERCIFUL LOVING-KINDNESS

As he sat at dinner in the house, many tax collectors and sinners came and were sitting with him and his disciples. When the Pharisees saw this, they said to his disciples, "Why does your teacher eat with tax collectors and sinners?" But when he heard this, he said, "Those who are well have no need of a physician, but those who are sick. Go and learn what this means, 'I desire mercy, not sacrifice.' "

MATTHEW 9:10–13

Since Jesus was steeped in the Scriptures that we read as the Old Testament, it is no surprise that he used them in his preaching and teaching. Matthew's Gospel presents Jesus twice quoting Hosea 6:6 in order to make a point: here to defend his practice of associating with sinners, and again to criticize some Pharisees' quickness to condemn (Matthew 12:7). Since Jesus twice quoted the words, "I desire mercy, not sacrifice" (Hosea 6:6), we too should "go and learn what this means."

We can note that Matthew's Gospel was written in Greek, and that Matthew therefore has Jesus quoting a Greek translation of the words of Hosea. In this translation it is "mercy" that God desires, using the same Greek word for mercy that Jesus will use in the beatitude, "Blessed are the merciful, for they will receive mercy" (Matthew 5:7).

If we look up Hosea 6:6 in our Bibles, however, we will find that most translations speak not of mercy but of love as God's desire: "For I desire steadfast love and not sacrifice." The Hebrew word that Hosea uses to express what God desires carries a broad range of meaning: It can be translated as love, kindness, mercy, grace, goodness, favor and benevolence. When the book of Hosea was translated into Greek, the Greek word for "mercy" was chosen to express what Hosea had said in Hebrew. But Hosea's Hebrew word carries a far broader meaning than "mercy," and we should keep this broader range of meaning in mind.

Hosea's first listeners would have immediately grasped what it was that God was asking for: He was asking them to have the same loving-kindness toward him that he had toward them. On Mount Sinai God proclaimed that he was "merciful and gracious, slow to anger, and abounding in steadfast love and faithfulness" (Exodus 34:6), and it was precisely this steadfast love that God was in turn demanding from his people through his prophet Hosea. One translation of Hosea 6:6 even renders it, "I desire loyalty, not sacrifice," making it clear that the love that God asks for is first of all our love for him.[1]

However, our love of God in return for his love must overflow into love for all those he loves. God asks us to behave toward others as he behaves toward us. As we receive his kindness, mercy and love, so we must be kind, merciful and loving to others.

This was what Jesus was inviting the Pharisees to reflect on in the two encounters in which he quoted the words of Hosea to them. The Pharisees took great pains to carry out what they understood to be the obligations God had imposed on them. But some of them overlooked something very basic: God's merciful loving-kindness toward us is a call to have the same merciful loving-kindness toward each other.

When Jesus welcomed sinners to him and ate with them, he was carrying out his Father's work, for his Father was a God of great mercy and loving-kindness. When some Pharisees criticized Jesus for associating with sinners, or when they harshly judged the disciples for foraging grain on the Sabbath (Matthew 12:7), they showed that they understood neither the merciful kindness of God nor how they were to reflect this merciful kindness in their own attitudes and actions.

FOR REFLECTION

What are the implications for me of God's valuing love more highly than sacrifice? How does Jesus' example show me the meaning of love?

JESUS GAVE ALMS

Jesus said to him [Judas], "Do quickly what you are going to do." Now no one at the table knew why he said this to him. Some thought that, because Judas had the common purse, Jesus was telling him, "Buy what we need for the festival"; or, that he should give something to the poor.

JOHN 13:27–29

When the sun is in the sky, we cannot see the stars, even though the heavens are as filled with stars by day as by night. So too in our reading of Scripture: We inevitably focus on the main characters and actions in a scene and miss details. When we read of Jesus' interaction with Judas during the Last Supper, our attention is on Judas' betrayal, and we probably do not dwell on Judas' role as keeper of the common purse. Yet this role reveals something significant about Jesus, if we reflect on it in light of other Gospel passages.

Luke tells us that Jesus and the twelve disciples were accompanied on their travels by some women, including Mary Magdalene, "Joanna, the wife of Herod's steward Chuza, and Susanna, and many others, who provided for them out of their resources" (Luke 8:3). Joanna at least would have been wealthy: Her husband was the chief administrator for Herod Antipas, the ruler of Galilee. Other disciples of Jesus also had resources that they put at the disposal of Jesus.

These contributions were held in a common purse and used to meet expenses. Jesus did not multiply food every time someone was hungry; usually food was purchased, as is implied in John 13:29. But that was not the only use made of funds in the common purse: Money was also given to the poor as alms. This emerges in the two passages that touch on Judas' role as keeper of the common purse.

When Mary of Bethany anointed Jesus' feet with a liter of costly perfumed oil, Judas complained: "Why was this perfume not sold for three hundred denarii and the money given to the poor?" (John 12:5). His complaint sounds as if it was not uncommon for items to be donated to Jesus, for them to be sold for cash and for the proceeds to be given to the poor. John's Gospel adds the observation that Judas "said this not because he cared about the poor, but because he was a thief; he kept the common purse and used to steal what was put into it" (John 12:6). The fact remains, however, that donations to Jesus were often used to help the poor as well as to provide for Jesus and his followers.

The same point emerges during the Last Supper: When Jesus sent Judas off, the others assumed it was either to buy something for their meal or to give alms to the poor. Those were Judas' normal duties as Jesus' treasurer.

The import of this is that Jesus not only taught the importance of almsgiving—of giving money to the poor—but also gave alms from what was at his disposal. This should not surprise us: Jesus would not ask his followers to do anything that he did not do himself. And he repeatedly did instruct his disciples to help the poor. "Sell your possessions, and give alms," he told them (Luke 12:33). "Sell what you own, and give the money to the poor," he told a rich man who was seeking eternal life (Mark 10:21). Jesus commended Zacchaeus for giving half of his possessions to the poor (Luke 19:8–9). Would Jesus be any less generous than he taught others to be? Jesus not only proclaimed good news to the poor (Luke 4:18; 7:22); he also expressed his love by helping them financially.

It might seem to us that his almsgiving was of minor importance compared with his inaugurating the kingdom of God through his teachings and healings. Yet it has this importance for us: Each of us is able to imitate his almsgiving even if we are not gifted to heal the sick or do the other mighty works of Jesus. Through word and example Jesus asks us to use what is at our disposal to assist those in need: It is part of our imitation of Christ.

FOR REFLECTION

How might I assist those in need? How much of my income and resources do I use to relieve the suffering of others?

THE GOOD SHEPHERD

I am the good shepherd. The good shepherd lays down his life for the sheep.... My sheep hear my voice. I know them, and they follow me. I give them eternal life, and they will never perish. No one will snatch them out of my hand. What my Father has given me is greater than all else, and no one can snatch it out of the Father's hand.

JOHN 10:11, 27–29

Jesus told us that he is the Good Shepherd, and he referred to us as sheep. No doubt his first audience was a lot more familiar with sheep than we are and found immediate meaning in his words. But what are we to learn from them?

Perhaps a good starting point is the parable of the one lost sheep in chapter 15 of Luke's Gospel (Luke 15:3–7). When this single animal wandered away from the flock, the shepherd left his other ninety-nine sheep and went looking for it until he found it. Jesus told this parable as a teaching about God's love for us and his readiness to forgive us; in the same chapter of Luke we find the parable of the Prodigal Son.

What is noteworthy is that the shepherd did not wait for the lost sheep to discover that it was lost and return to the flock. Rather the shepherd went after the stray, even though he had ninety-nine other sheep to be concerned about.

Our understanding of repentance is usually slightly different. We tend to think that when we sin, God sits back and waits for us to come to our senses and return to him, begging forgiveness. But that is not how Jesus portrayed this shepherd. He told us that the shepherd searched for the lost sheep, searching until he found it and brought it back to the flock.

That is the kind of shepherd Jesus is. He does not wait for us to come back to him; he takes the initiative to come after us when we have strayed. Our reconciliation begins with him.

Jesus also said that no one will snatch his sheep away from him (John 10:28). We can sometimes think of our lives as a gigantic struggle, with Jesus beckoning on one side and various forces of temptation and evil pulling us the other way. Jesus assures us that we are not going to be swept away as hapless victims of these forces. He has a claim on us and is not going to let go.

We can certainly turn our backs on Jesus and reject him; he does not take away our free will. But he is not going to stand idly by while forces of evil overpower us. The power of Jesus is greater than the forces that oppose him, because the power of Jesus is the power of God himself. No one can snatch his disciples out of his hand, because no one can snatch them out of his Father's hand (John 10:29).

Jesus' determination to save us and give us eternal life is very good news for us. It is such good news that we might have trouble completely believing it, conditioned as we are to doubt all the claims that are too good to be true.

But Jesus gives us incontrovertible evidence of the truth of his teaching about God's mercy toward us. He tells us that he is a good shepherd who lays down his life for his sheep. His dying to redeem us is the proof of how serious he is about saving us and reclaiming us when we are lost. "God proves his love for us in that while we still were still sinners Christ died for us" (Romans 5:8).

Could Jesus have done anything more to prove his love for us and to demonstrate his determination that we not be lost? If he was willing to die for us, would he not be willing to search us out when we stray? If he has already given up his life for us so that we might have eternal life, will he not now do all in his power to preserve eternal life in us?

Which of Jesus' teachings speaks most strongly to me about his love for me? How in the events of my life has Jesus demonstrated his love?

LIVING WATER

> *On the last day of the festival, the great day,*
> *while Jesus was standing there, he cried out, "Let*
> *anyone who is thirsty come to me, and let the*
> *one who believes in me drink. As the scripture*
> *has said, 'Out of the believer's heart shall flow*
> *rivers of living water.' " Now he said this about*
> *the Spirit, which believers in him were to receive.*

JOHN 7:37–39

The setting is the temple in Jerusalem, during the Feast of Tabernacles. On each of the seven days of the feast, water was drawn from the Gihon Spring, lying southeast of the temple in the Kidron Valley. This water was carried in procession into the temple and poured over the altar. On the last day, when the celebration reached its climax, Jesus stood up in the temple precincts and proclaimed himself the true source of living water—a proclamation that John sees as the fulfillment of Old Testament prophecy.

But to what prophecy is John referring here? No Old Testament prophecy exactly matches the words John uses, but several convey the essential thought. One important passage for understanding the significance of Jesus' words is from the prophet Ezekiel (Ezekiel 47:1–12).

Ezekiel had a vision of a spring gushing forth from the Holy of Holies in the temple, flowing past the altar, out of the temple compound and into the Kidron Valley. As it flows through the valley it grows from a shallow brook only ankle deep to a stream waist-deep, then finally becomes a mighty river impossible to cross. Everywhere this river flows, trees spring to life along its banks, and "they will bear fresh fruit every month, because the water for them flows from the sanctuary" (Ezekiel 47:12). Not only is the fruit good to eat, but the leaves of the trees cure illness. Finally the river empties into the Dead Sea, making its brackish water wholesome. Fish begin to live in the sea, as plentifully as in the Mediterranean (Ezekiel 47:10).

This is a remarkable vision in itself. Normally a spring is strongest and purest at its mouth, and the farther its water flows the more it evaporates or is absorbed into the ground. But the living water in Ezekiel's vision grows mightier as it flows.

Further, the countryside between Jerusalem and the Dead Sea is a desolate wilderness, rocky and incapable of sustaining much life. But as this stream flows through it life springs forth, life that no normal water could sustain.

Finally, when the stream reaches the Dead Sea, it transforms that sea. This contrasts with the Jordan River, whose waters are pure but become swallowed up by the brackish waters of the Dead Sea after the Jordan empties into it.

When Ezekiel proclaimed this vision, it was a message of the power of God. God's grace brings life to what is barren, even as this stream from the temple brings life wherever it goes. God's grace overcomes seemingly insurmountable obstacles, even as this stream conquers the desolate Judean wilderness and the salty Dead Sea.

This prophecy of Ezekiel was one of the passages read during the Feast of Tabernacles. When Jesus stood up and cried out, he was proclaiming that he was the source of the living water that Ezekiel had foretold. He was the new temple (John 2:19–21), from which would flow the living water of eternal life that he had promised to the woman at the well (John 4:10–14). From him would issue a mighty, growing stream, bringing salvation wherever it went. John adds that Jesus was speaking of the Spirit, whom all who believed in Jesus were to receive. Jesus in his love for us sends us the Holy Spirit.

Ezekiel's vision of the stream helps us understand something of the work and power of the Spirit. To be touched by the Spirit is to be transformed. No matter how barren we are in ourselves, the Spirit can bring us to life. No matter how overwhelming our difficulties may appear, the Spirit has the power to overcome them.

When a visitor to the Holy Land follows the Kidron Valley down to the Dead Sea, the desolation of the area is overwhelming, and it appears that nothing could ever grow there. It seems impossible that fish could survive in the lifeless waters. Yet the living water that issues from Jesus can bring life to even more desolate areas of our soul. The Holy Spirit, whom he gives, can transform us and give us abundant life.

FOR REFLECTION

How am I most aware of the presence of the Holy Spirit in my life? Where am I most in need of the Spirit's transforming power?

THE DEPTH OF HIS LOVE

Father, forgive them; for they do not know
what they are doing.

LUKE 23:34

Jesus' love is nowhere more apparent than during the last days of his earthly life.

Jesus traveled to Jerusalem knowing that suffering and death awaited him there (Luke 9:22, 44, 51; 13:33; 18:31–33). Yet he wept over the city because it would be destroyed (Luke 19:41–44). Jesus loved his friend Lazarus and wept at his death (John 11:35–36); Jesus also wept at the suffering in store for the city that would crucify him. The Gospels tell us of only these two instances of Jesus weeping—once for a beloved friend, once for enemies. "Love your enemies," Jesus commanded (Luke 6:27). He was asking us to be as concerned about the well-being of those who harm us as those who love us; he was asking us to imitate his example.

The Fourth Eucharistic Prayer of the Mass proclaims, "He always loved those who were his own in the world. When the time came for him to be glorified by you, his heavenly Father, he showed the depths of his love." On the night before he died, Jesus gave his followers bread as his body, "which is given for you," and wine as his blood "that is poured out for you" (Luke 22:19–20). Jesus apparently gave his body and blood even to Judas (Luke 22:21–23). Jesus would give up his life for everyone: for disciples who squabbled during this solemn meal (Luke 22:24–27); for Peter, who would deny him (Luke 22:34); even for Judas, who would betray him.

Jesus knew that he would suffer horribly and be put to death if he fell into the hands of his enemies, and the prospect filled him with anguish (Luke 22:44). Yet he prayed to his

Father, "Not my will but yours be done" (Luke 22:42). When a mob arrived to arrest him, Jesus would not let his followers defend him and thus spare him from suffering; he even healed a man they wounded (Luke 22:50–51). "Do not resist an evil-doer," Jesus had commanded (Matthew 5:39). Jesus did not resist arrest; he instead healed one of his captors.

Even after Jesus had been horribly scourged and was being led out to be crucified, his concern was not for himself but for others. He told the women of Jerusalem, "Do not weep for me, but weep for yourselves and for your children," again thinking of the coming destruction of the city (Luke 23:28). Raised up on the cross, Jesus made no reply to the mockery of the executioners and the crowd; he responded only to a criminal who was being executed beside him. This criminal admitted that he deserved crucifixion but that Jesus didn't, and he asked Jesus, "Remember me when you come into your kingdom" (Luke 23:42). Jesus promised him that he would join him in paradise that very day (Luke 23:43).

The depth of Jesus' love is revealed in his prayer from the cross, "Father, forgive them; for they do not know what they are doing." Jesus had taught, "Forgive, if you have anything against anyone" (Mark 11:25). What greater grievance could a person have than that against those who were torturing him to death? Yet Jesus not only forgave them; he asked his Father to forgive them. "Pray for those who abuse you," Jesus had commanded (Luke 6:28), and now he prayed for those who were crucifying him. Jesus pleaded ignorance as a mitigating factor, as a defense lawyer might plead to a judge on behalf of a guilty client. Jesus became the advocate for those who crucified him—such is the depth of his love.

If Jesus forgave and prayed for those who were putting him to death, will he not have the same love for us? We can "approach the throne of grace with boldness, so that we may receive mercy" (Hebrews 4:16), for Jesus "is at the right hand of God" and "intercedes for us" (Romans 8:34). It is as if the cross reached up to heaven and placed Jesus at God's right hand as our advocate. There he pleads for us, out of his depth of love for us.

For Reflection

Read Luke's account of Jesus' last twenty-four hours before his death (chapters 22 and 23 of his Gospel). Ponder the passages that speak to you most strongly about the depth of Jesus' love for you, and respond in prayer.

THREE

THE FRIENDS OF JESUS

I have called you friends.

TAX COLLECTORS

As Jesus was walking along, he saw a man called Matthew sitting at the tax booth; and he said to him, "Follow me." And he got up and followed him.

And as he sat at dinner in the house, many tax collectors and sinners were sitting with him and his disciples. When the Pharisees saw this, they said to his disciples, "Why does your teacher eat with tax collectors and sinners?"

MATTHEW 9:9–11

Tax collectors were an object of scorn at the time of Jesus, spoken of in the same breath with sinners. Tax collectors were agents, directly or indirectly, of Rome. Rome had conquered Palestine in 63 BC and imposed taxes. Every tax payment reminded Jews that they were under Roman rule, and they despised those who collected taxes on behalf of Rome.

The tax system lent itself to abuse. It was common for Rome to auction off the right to collect taxes and then allow the high bidder to keep anything he could collect over the amount he bid. It was a green light for greed, and many tax collectors took full advantage of it. Hence John the Baptist admonished tax collectors, "Collect no more than the amount prescribed for you" (Luke 3:13).

There were many forms of taxation, and together they extracted a sizeable portion of the income of ordinary people—up to 40 percent by one estimate. As a result tax collectors were considered unscrupulous extortionists working for a foreign power who drained people's livelihoods.

Matthew is described as "sitting at the tax booth" (Matthew 9:9) outside Capernaum. A duty was imposed on merchandise at border crossings. Philip governed the territory east of the Jordan River, and Herod Antipas governed the territory to the west, both ruling on behalf of Rome. Capernaum had a customs post because it lay on a trade route from Damascus, and it was the first town on this route west of the Jordan River.

Matthew was an agent of Herod Antipas, collecting duties on merchandise entering his realm. Working for Herod Antipas would have been another mark against Matthew: This was the Herod Antipas who had married his brother's wife, executed John the Baptist and wanted to kill Jesus (Mark 6:17–29; Luke 13:31).

It is little wonder then that those attending a dinner with Matthew are described as "tax collectors and sinners"—they were probably the only people willing to accept an invitation to eat at his house.

Except for Jesus.

Jesus was not ashamed to associate with tax collectors and other outcasts. He was even viewed as "a friend of tax collectors and sinners" (Matthew 11:19). Why didn't having tax collectors as friends bother Jesus?

For one thing, Jesus had nothing against paying taxes to Rome: "Give therefore to the emperor the things that are the emperor's, and to God the things that are God's" (Matthew 22:21). Jesus came to inaugurate the kingdom of God, not to replace Roman rule by Jewish rule.

For another thing, Jesus recognized that there could be honorable people in despised occupations. Zacchaeus was such a person: a "chief tax collector" (Luke 19:2) who gave half of his income to the poor and made fourfold restitution to anyone he defrauded (Luke 19:8 is best translated in the present tense, as an indication of what Zacchaeus was already doing).

But most importantly, Jesus came to bring salvation to everyone, tax collectors as well as fishermen. He no more held himself aloof from sinners than a doctor avoided sick people: "Those who are well have no need of a physician, but those who are sick do" (Matthew 9:12).

There is both comfort and challenge for us in the example of Jesus. He does not hold himself aloof from us, no matter who we are. But he asks us to likewise go out to the outcasts, recognizing the goodness that is in them and bringing them his mercy and message.

FOR REFLECTION

What can I learn from Jesus' choice of the people with whom he associated? From his welcoming those who were rejected by others?

JESUS' PATRONS

*[Jesus] went on through cities and villages,
proclaiming and bringing the good news of the
kingdom of God. The twelve were with him, as
well as some women who had been cured of evil
spirits and infirmities: Mary, called Magdalene,
from whom seven demons had gone out, and
Joanna, the wife of Herod's steward Chuza, and
Susanna, and many others, who provided for
them out of their resources.*

LUKE 8:1–3

Luke tells us that a group of women traveled with Jesus and financially supported him and the disciples. Luke names three of these women—perhaps because they were the major donors. What can we learn about, and from, these women?

Joanna was married to Chuza, who managed the vast estates of Herod Antipas, the ruler of Galilee. Chuza had a position of considerable importance and income. Joanna and Chuza likely lived in Tiberias, Herod's capital on the shore of the Sea of Galilee. Joanna and Chuza were part of the wealthy elite.

"Mary, called Magdalene" is not to be identified with the sinful woman of chapter 7 of Luke; popular piety was mistaken in making her a repentant prostitute. Mary came from the city of Magdala, three miles north of Tiberias. Magdala was a major fish-processing center, where fish were salted to preserve them for export. It had a harbor and shipyards, making it an important commercial center.

Was Mary called Magdalene simply to distinguish her from other Marys? Or did this indicate that she was a business-woman of Magdala, perhaps involved in wholesaling fish? Some upper-class women of the time conducted such businesses.

(Men usually ran things in the ancient world, but there were exceptions.) We can suspect that Mary's financial means derived from the flourishing industry and trade of Magdala.

Susanna we know little about, save that Luke includes her among the women whom Jesus healed and who financially supported him. This is the only mention of her in the New Testament.

In the society of the time, Joanna, Mary Magdalene and Susanna would have been considered patrons of Jesus. A patron was a person of influence or wealth who assisted someone of lesser status. Lydia, a businesswoman and household head in Philippi, acted as Paul's patron (Acts 16:12–15, 40). Our turning to "patron saints" for help is an echo of the ancient practice of patronage.

But Joanna, Mary and Susanna were more than patrons of Jesus; they were also his disciples. The Gospels nowhere mention Jesus entering Tiberias or Magdala; presumably these women sought Jesus out, to be "cured of evil spirits and infirmities." In Luke's Gospel Jesus' casting out of evil spirits is often linked with physical or mental disorders (Luke 4:40–41; 6:18; 9:38–42; 11:14; 13:11–13). These women came to Jesus with their afflictions, and he healed them.

Thereafter they were his disciples, and they used their financial means to support him and the other disciples. They were faithful disciples to the very end: Even when other disciples abandoned Jesus, they kept vigil at the cross and saw his burial (Luke 23:49, 55). Later these women returned to his tomb, bringing spices to anoint his body (Luke 23:56; 24:1). Burial spices could be expensive (John 12:3–7); this was their final act of using their financial means for Jesus. The tomb was empty, and Mary Magdalene and Joanna and other women were the first witnesses of his resurrection (Luke 24:2–10).

It is fitting that we remember Mary Magdalene and the other women for their faithfulness to the end and their encounter with the Risen Christ. But their lives also have other lessons for us. They turned to Jesus in their need, risking the sneers of their upper-class friends. They gave their lives to Jesus, leaving behind the comforts of their status. They used their money to support Jesus and his mission. In the eyes of the world they were Jesus' patrons; in their own eyes they were his disciples, giving themselves and their resources to him, out of gratitude for what he had done for them. We are invited to do likewise.

FOR REFLECTION

What example do the women who followed and helped Jesus set for me? How might those who were patrons of Jesus serve as patron saints for me?

THE NEW FAMILY OF JESUS

Then his mother and his brothers came; and standing outside, they sent to him and called him. A crowd was sitting around him; and they said to him, "Your mother and your brothers and sisters are outside, asking for you." And he replied, "Who are my mother and my brothers?" And looking at those who sat round him, he said, "Here are my mother and my brothers! Whoever does the will of God is my brother and sister and mother."

MARK 3:31–35

Jesus' apparent rejection of his family in favor of his disciples can perplex us. What is going on here?

If we find Jesus' behavior perplexing, it was outright shocking back in the first century. Family relationships counted for a good deal more in the culture of the time than they do in the modern world. One's identity was bound up in one's kinship. Family obligations took precedence over personal achievement in a way we, in our culture of individualism, have a hard time fathoming.

One trivial example of this culture gap: Sometimes when I am making a financial transaction, I am asked for my mother's maiden name as proof of my identity, on the assumption that no one else would know it. But in the villages of Jesus' time, everyone would know everyone else's mother's maiden name, as well as their genealogy for a few generations back. One's family was one's identity.

It was therefore shocking for Jesus to apparently turn his back on his family. It was also shocking for Jesus to demand that a disciple follow him immediately instead of fulfilling the solemn obligation of burying his father (Matthew 8:21–22). It was shocking for Jesus to say that those who heard the word of God and kept it were blessed, rather than the mother who bore and nursed him (Luke 11:27–28).

It was shocking for Jesus to put loyalty to him above family loyalties: "Whoever loves father or mother more than me is not worthy of me; and whoever loves son or daughter more than me is not worthy of me" (Matthew 10:37; see also Matthew 10:34–36). Jesus promised great rewards for those who set aside their family relationships for his sake (Mark 10:29–30). Jesus seemingly challenged one of the bedrock institutions of the culture in which he lived.

How is all this to be understood? Clearly, Jesus was not anti-family or deficient in his love for his mother. There must be something more going on. And that indeed is the key:

"something more." As important as family ties are, Jesus was offering something more. He was creating a new family, a new web of relationships centered on himself. He was offering a new identity to those who follow him, based on their incorporation into his new family. He was offering adoption into the family of God, so that his Father would become our Father, making us brothers and sisters of Jesus and one another.

Becoming part of this new family established by Jesus is of such great consequence that our normal relationships pale in comparison—even relationships like husband and wife, father and daughter, mother and son. All of these relationships are good and part of God's plan, but they are also all meant to be taken up into kinship in the new family of Jesus.

What about Mary, who was standing outside that day asking for Jesus? If the criteria for membership in the new family of Jesus is doing the will of God, then Mary is the preeminent member. Luke clarifies this in his account of the incident, for he presents Jesus saying, "My mother and my brothers are those who hear the word and do it" (Luke 8:21; Luke 11:27–28 should be similarly interpreted).

Our shock over Jesus' words about family relationships should turn to gratitude. He is not telling us to reject our families but offering us something even better than the love we experience in them. He is inviting us to become part of his family; he is calling us into kinship with himself and his Father.

For Reflection

What has life been like for me in the family of Jesus' followers? With whom do I feel the closest bond?

THE TWELVE

Now during those days he went out to the
mountain to pray; and he spent the night in
prayer to God. And when day came, he called
his disciples and chose twelve of them, whom
he also named apostles: Simon, whom he
named Peter, and his brother Andrew, and
James, and John, and Philip, and Bartholomew,
and Matthew, and Thomas, and James son of
Alphaeus, and Simon, who was called the
Zealot, and Judas son of James, and Judas
Iscariot, who became a traitor.

LUKE 6:12–16

What went through the minds of the twelve when Jesus chose them to be apostles? Perhaps awe that they were chosen, perhaps excitement over what lay ahead. And perhaps as well, some uneasiness as they glanced at who else had been chosen and wondered, "Am I expected to get along with *these* people?"

Matthew was a tax collector (Matthew 10:3), an occupation that lent itself to corruption. Many devout Jews held themselves aloof from tax collectors as sinners (Mark 2:16). Were some of the twelve uncomfortable with Matthew's presence in their midst? We might suspect that in particular Simon, "who was called the Zealot," had problems with Matthew. Simon was most likely called "the Zealot" because he was very zealous about observing the law of Moses and insisting that others obey it (a violent revolutionary group called the Zealots would not form until the Jewish rebellion against Rome in AD 66–70). What did Simon the Zealot think of Matthew—and was Matthew comfortable in the presence of this zealot?

James and John were known as "Sons of Thunder" (Mark 3:17), likely indicating a stormy disposition; they were the ones who wanted to call down fire from heaven on a Samaritan village (Luke 9:54). They jockeyed for positions of power and honor among the twelve (Mark 10:35–37), leading the other apostles to become indignant (Mark 10:41). How easy was it to put up with these self-seeking "Sons of Thunder" day after day?

And what did the other eleven think of Judas Iscariot? He was the keeper of their common purse but a thief (John 12:6). Did the rest of the apostles catch on to his pilfering? If so, what impact did this have on their relationship with him?

The twelve seem a collection of people unlikely to get along very well with one another. Yet Jesus chose them after spending an entire night in prayer seeking his Father's will (Luke 6:12). Perhaps one lesson is this: Jesus doesn't choose his followers on the basis of their compatibility with one another. Rather he chooses whom he chooses and then teaches them how to behave as his disciples. If they carry out his teaching, then harmony can reign even in the most unlikely of groupings.

"Love your enemies," Jesus taught (Matthew 5:44). You there, Simon the Zealot, you must love Matthew the tax collector—and you, Matthew, you must love Simon, who thinks you don't measure up to God's standards.

"Whoever wants to be first must be last of all and servant of all" (Mark 9:35). Did you hear that, James and John? And as for the rest of you: Are you indignant over the request of James and John because you want these places of honor for yourself?

"You cannot serve God and wealth" (Luke 16:13). Are you listening, Judas Iscariot?

"Just as I have loved you, you also should love one another" (John 13:34). That was Jesus' command to all of them. He loved those he had chosen, despite their faults, despite their many failures to understand him, despite however they might betray or deny him. They were to love one another with an equally resolute love.

If we chafe over the groupings in which we find ourselves— family or parish, neighborhood or work—then perhaps our chafing is a clue that we need to hear the words of Jesus more clearly and heed them more carefully. Perhaps Jesus chose twelve who wouldn't naturally get along with one another so they could serve as an example for us, teaching us how to love those we are not naturally inclined to love.

FOR REFLECTION

Would I have felt at home with the apostles if Jesus had chosen me as a thirteenth? Who would I have had the easiest time relating to? Who might have raised my hackles?

THE MAN IN THE TREE

[Jesus] entered Jericho and was passing through it. A man was there named Zacchaeus; he was a chief tax collector and was rich. He was trying to see who Jesus was, but on account of the crowd he could not, because he was short in stature. So he ran ahead and climbed a sycamore tree to see him, because he was going to pass that way. When Jesus came to the place, he looked up and said to him, "Zacchaeus, hurry and come down; for I must stay at your house today."

LUKE 19:1–5

The much-despised tax collectors of the Gospels were often customs collectors, stationed along trade routes. Matthew worked at a tax booth on the highway that passed by Capernaum (Matthew 9:9). Jericho lay at the intersection of north-south and east-west trade routes; as "a chief tax collector," Zacchaeus was likely in charge of collecting customs from caravans that passed through.

The Romans commonly auctioned off positions such as that held by Zacchaeus. The tax system lent itself to tax collectors' extracting as much in taxes as they could. It is little surprise that being in charge of customs in a crossroads town like Jericho made Zacchaeus a rich man.

What is surprising is that he would climb a tree in order to get a glimpse of Jesus. In a culture that prized dignity and honor, the sight of wealthy Zacchaeus in a tree would have brought howls of derision from the crowd. Zacchaeus apparently didn't care: He wanted to see Jesus.

Zacchaeus's disregard for his dignity impressed Jesus, and Jesus apparently changed his plans: instead of passing through Jericho on his way to Jerusalem, he invited himself into the home of Zacchaeus. This amazed the crowd even more than the sight of Zacchaeus up a tree: "He has gone to be the guest of one who is a sinner" (Luke 19:7). Tax collectors were despised as sinners because of their occupation, and devout Jews avoided contact with them. This was not the first time, however, that Jesus caused consternation because of those with whom he chose to associate (see Luke 5:29–30; 15:1–2).

What happened next is a matter of disagreement among biblical scholars and translators. Many translations have Zacchaeus saying, "Half of my possessions, Lord, I will give to the poor; and if I have defrauded anyone of anything, I will pay back four times as much" (Luke 19:8). This makes the story of

Zacchaeus a conversion story: After meeting Jesus he pledges to give away half of his wealth to those in need and make fourfold restitution for what he has extorted.

However, the Greek text of Luke's Gospel has Zacchaeus speaking of what he already was doing rather than what he intended to do, and some scholars maintain that the proper translation of his words should be, "I give away half of my possessions to the poor; if I have defrauded anyone of anything, I pay back four times as much." If this is the proper way to understand Zacchaeus's words, then Jesus' response to them is a recognition of the good that is in Zacchaeus and an affirmation of him as "a son of Abraham" (Luke 19:9). Zacchaeus already was a long way toward doing what Jesus had invited the rich young man to do: use his wealth to help the poor (Luke 18:22).

The story of Zacchaeus is rich in lessons for us. The man in the tree poses the question, are we eager enough to meet Jesus that we are willing to set aside our pretenses and self-concerns? And whether Jesus commended Zacchaeus for what he was already doing or for what he intended to do, in either case we are invited to imitate Zacchaeus's generosity toward those in need and the restitution he made for his wrongdoing.

If the story of Zacchaeus is interpreted as Jesus' seeing good in a man others despised, then it poses an additional challenge. Are there those whom we scorn but whom Jesus would honor? Does Jesus invite us to acknowledge their goodness?

For Reflection

What would have been my attitude toward Zacchaeus before his encounter with Jesus? How can I better imitate his eagerness to see Jesus? His generosity with his money?

TWO DISCIPLES

Mary took a pound of costly perfume made of pure nard, anointed Jesus' feet, and wiped them with her hair. The house was filled with the fragrance of the perfume. But Judas Iscariot, one of his disciples (the one who was about to betray him), said, "Why was this perfume not sold for three hundred denarii and the money given to the poor?" (He said this not because he cared about the poor, but because he was a thief; he kept the common purse and used to steal what was put into it.)

JOHN 12:3–6

Each of the Gospels has a scene in which a woman anointed Jesus (Matthew 26:6–13; Mark 14:3–9; Luke 7:36–50; John 12:1–8). While it is interesting to compare the different accounts, each should also be read and understood on its own.

In the Gospel of John, the woman who anointed Jesus was Mary of Bethany, the sister of Martha and Lazarus. Jesus interpreted her anointing in terms of his coming burial (John 12:7), but it is not clear that Mary was aware of this significance of her deed. She may have anointed his feet with perfumed oil simply as a gesture of love.

And what a gesture it was! The perfumed oil was worth "three hundred denarii"—a year's wages for an ordinary worker. There is no evidence that Mary, Martha or Lazarus was wealthy; the Gospels present them as ordinary people. They were able to offer Jesus a meal when he visited, but it was a meal that Martha prepared, probably indicating that they had no servants (Luke 10:38–42).

It was, therefore, quite an extravagance for Mary to pour a year's wages worth of perfumed oil on Jesus' feet. Her act might have meant her using up her life's savings in one great gesture of love. We could compare it to finding a pearl of great price and selling everything in order to buy it—and then giving this pearl to Jesus (see Matthew 13:45–46).

Judas also played a role in this incident. Whenever we think of Judas, we think of him as the one who betrayed Jesus. But he had not done so yet. When Mary anointed Jesus, Judas was still one of the twelve who had been specially chosen by Jesus. He had even been entrusted with responsibility for the common fund that was used for expenses and helping the poor (see John 13:29). To an outside observer Judas was not only one of the twelve but one of the leaders among the twelve.

Tragically he abused his position by stealing from the common fund. His words of concern for the poor were hypocritical: He simply wanted more money to flow into the common purse so that he could divert more into his own pocket. His greed would ultimately lead him to ask the enemies of Jesus, "What will you give me if I betray him to you?" (Matthew 26:15).

What a contrast! One disciple gave to Jesus with reckless abandon; another disciple stole from Jesus and from the poor. One had no thought for herself but only for the Jesus she loved. The other thought only of himself and of how he could use the position Jesus had given him for his own gain.

Most of us are not as generous as Mary, nor are we as grasping as Judas. Yet the same impulses that moved their hearts can move ours. On the one hand, there may be a bit of Judas in us. However pure our intentions once might have been, we may find ourselves taking more than we give, using any status we have for our own benefit, capitalizing on our following of Christ for our own advantage. If we do not curb our self-seeking, our discipleship may be extinguished, as was the discipleship of Judas.

On the other hand, we may also have an impulse to give all to Jesus, to gather up everything we own and everything we are in one bundle and lay it at his feet. That is the impulse of God's grace in us. Mary of Bethany can be our model, a model of giving to Jesus with abandon, of giving ourselves totally to him.

FOR REFLECTION

What warning does the example of Judas hold for me? What inspiration does the woman who anointed Jesus have for me?

THOSE WHOM YOU GAVE ME

*I am asking on their behalf; I am not asking
on behalf of the world, but on behalf of those
whom you gave me, because they are yours. All
mine are yours, and yours are mine; and I
have been glorified in them. And now I am no
longer in the world, but they are in the world,
and I am coming to you. Holy Father, protect
them in your name that you have given me, so
that they may be one, as we are one. While I
was with them, I protected them in your name
that you have given me.*

JOHN 17:9–12

The Gospel of John presents us with a long prayer of Jesus at the close of the Last Supper. Jesus prayed for his disciples, his closest friends, who were sharing this most sacred meal with him. But in his prayer he did not refer to them as his disciples or friends, although they most certainly were (see John 15:15, for example). Jesus instead prayed to his Father for "those whom you gave me."

Jesus put the accent on the disciples' being chosen by and belonging to the Father, rather than on their having been chosen by him and belonging to him. Jesus acknowledged that the disciples were the Father's gift to him, rather than his own achievement. He saw the disciples as belonging to him only in the sense that he shared all the Father had, and they first belonged to the Father. "They were yours, and you gave them to me" (John 17:6).

Luke gives us a glimpse of this same reality when he presents the selection of the twelve: "Now during those days he went out to the mountain to pray; and he spent the night in prayer to God. And when day came, he called his disciples and chose twelve of them, whom he also named apostles" (Luke 6:12–13).

Jesus did not merely pray for God's guidance in the important matter of choosing the twelve. Rather he asked in prayer who his Father had chosen and was entrusting to him. The difference may be subtle, but it is important: it is the difference between asking someone for his advice in a certain matter and asking him what decision he has made in the matter.

Jesus' attitude toward his followers has an application in our lives. Although our relationship with the Father is different from that of Jesus, we participate in his sonship and can truly consider ourselves children of God. We can also consider those with whom we have a special relationship to be those whom God has given us: our spouse, our children, our parents, other members of our family, our friends, our coworkers.

These people are not a part of our lives because of any special revelation we have received from God; they are there because of choices we have made or because of circumstances, some of them accidental. But we can consider them to be those whom God has given us. Each of them is in our care in some way.

What is at issue is how we look at them. Do we consider the people in our lives to be satellites orbiting around us, existing at our pleasure and for our service? Or do we hold them as people who belong to God, as ones he has created and is redeeming, as those whom, in his providence, he has made a part of our lives and given us an opportunity to serve? Are they "my" family and friends, or are they children of God, loaned to my care?

The example of Jesus in his relationship with his disciples sets the pattern for us. He was concerned for his disciples' well-being, concerned to keep them true to their call from God. He taught them, and as is evident from John 17, he prayed for them.

Above all, Jesus loved those the Father had given him. He put up with their inconsistencies and failures; he did not draw back from loving them even when they betrayed him. He gave himself up for their sake, for they had been given to him by his Father. He invites us to do the same for those whom the Father has given us.

FOR REFLECTION

Whom has God given me to love and serve? How might I better cherish and care for them?

THE FIRST WITNESS

But Mary stood weeping outside the tomb.... Jesus said to her, "Mary!" She turned and said to him in Hebrew, "Rabbouni!" (which means Teacher). Jesus said to her, "Do not hold on to me, because I have not yet ascended to the Father. But go to my brothers and say to them, 'I am ascending to my Father and your Father,

to my God and your God.'" Mary Magdalene
went and announced to the disciples, "I have
seen the Lord."

JOHN 20:11, 16–18

Mary Magdalene is often thought of as something she was not and too infrequently remembered for what she was. The Bible nowhere describes Mary Magdalene as a prostitute. It does say that she was one of the women "who had been cured of evil spirits and infirmities" and that "seven demons had gone out" from her (Luke 8:2).

Could these seven demons have manifested themselves in sexual immorality? Jesus' casting out of demons is often linked with physical healings (Luke 4:40–41; 6:17–19), including the healing of such afflictions as muteness (Matthew 9:32–33) and curvature of the spine (Luke 13:11–13). In other cases demon possession caused mental disorders or convulsions (Mark 5:2–5; 9:17–29). But the Gospels describe no instance of Jesus expelling a demon that had led a woman into prostitution. Therefore, the plausible interpretation is that Mary Magdalene had been healed of some physical affliction by Jesus, even multiple afflictions.

How then did she enter into popular lore as a prostitute? In about the sixth century, she became identified with the unnamed woman "who was a sinner" who anointed Jesus' feet (Luke 7:36–50). But Luke does not make this identification; he introduces Mary Magdalene a few verses later as if for the first time (Luke 8:2), implying that these were different women.

Even if Mary Magdalene was this sinful woman, what basis is there for concluding that her sin was prostitution? Are women capable of no other sin? What does it say about one's view of women if one imagines that a woman's sins must be sexual in nature?

If Scripture does not portray Mary Magdalene as a prostitute, how does it portray her? She followed Jesus as he traveled about in Galilee; she was one of the women who used their own resources to take care of Jesus and of other disciples (Luke 8:1–3)—she was one of his patrons. She followed Jesus to Jerusalem, and she did not run away in his hour of crisis. She was a witness to the crucifixion and burial of Jesus (Mark 15:40–41, 47).

Most importantly, Mary Magdalene was a witness to the Resurrection of Jesus. Some disciples hid behind locked doors out of fear (John 20:19), but Mary Magdalene and a few other women bravely ventured forth on Easter morning, going out a gate of Jerusalem and past the hill of Calvary on their way to the tomb of Jesus (Mark 16:1–2). The tomb was empty, and an angel told the women that Jesus was risen from the dead (Mark 16:4–6).

In John's account Mary remained at the tomb, and the Risen Jesus appeared to her—the first to whom he manifested himself (John 20:11–18). The longer ending of Mark's Gospel preserves the same tradition: "Now after he rose early on the first day of the week, he appeared first to Mary Magdalene" (Mark 16:9). Mary Magdalene was commissioned to tell the other disciples about the Risen Lord (John 20:17).

How then does Scripture present Mary Magdalene to us? As one who was healed by Jesus and who supported him as his patron during his public ministry. As one who followed him to the end, even after others ran away. As one who was steadfast in her devotion to Jesus, even in his death, and became the first to see the Risen Lord. As the first commissioned to tell others that Jesus was raised—"the apostle to the apostles," as she has been called.

Mary Magdalene deserves a special place of honor among the followers of Jesus. She served him faithfully, and she was the first witness to his resurrection.

What has been my attitude toward Mary Magdalene? How am I able to imitate her love for and service of Jesus?

JESUS' SPECIAL FRIEND

When they had gone ashore, they saw a charcoal fire there, with fish on it, and bread.... Jesus said to them, "Come and have breakfast." ... When they had finished breakfast, Jesus said to Simon Peter, "Simon, son of John, do you love me more than these?" He said to him, "Yes, Lord; you know that I love you." Jesus said to him, "Feed my lambs."

JOHN 21:9, 12, 15

After his resurrection Jesus three times asked Peter if he loved him, giving Peter an opportunity to make amends for three times denying that he knew Jesus. After each assurance of Peter's love, Jesus asked Peter to care for his flock.

We understand this scene in light of Peter's being the leader of the twelve apostles, the rock on whom Jesus founded the church (Matthew 16:18–19). But there is another element to consider, in light of archaeology and the Gospels.

Archaeologists have found the lower walls of a first-century house in Capernaum that from every indication was Peter's home. It is a roughly twenty-by-twenty foot room that was built about 50 BC and used as an ordinary single-room house until the middle of the first century. Then its stone walls were plastered, and it was used for worship; petitions such as "Christ have mercy" were inscribed in the plaster. A pilgrim visited the site around the year 390 and noted in her diary, "In Capernaum a house church was made out of the house of Peter, and its walls still stand today."[1]

The Gospels mention this house. "As soon as they left the synagogue, they entered the house of Simon and Andrew," where Jesus cured Simon Peter's mother-in-law (Mark 1:29–31). This was the house where "the whole city was gathered around the door" with their sick (Mark 1:32–33). This was the house whose roof was broken open to allow the paralytic to be lowered to Jesus, who "was at home" (Mark 2:1–12).

Jesus made Capernaum the base of his public ministry in Galilee (Matthew 4:13), apparently staying with Peter (see also Mark 3:19). When Peter "came home" with the message that it was time to pay taxes, Jesus made provision for his taxes to be paid with Peter's, as if Jesus was a member of Peter's household (Matthew 17:24–27).

Jesus not only made Peter the first among the twelve (see Matthew 10:2); Jesus lived with Peter, sleeping in the same room with him. Jesus and Peter were close friends; they were family.

Once when I was guiding a group of pilgrims through Capernaum and explaining Peter's house and what it implies about Jesus' close relationship with Peter, one of the members of my group, Mary Heilman, exclaimed, "How it must have hurt Jesus when Peter denied him!" To have your best friend deny even knowing you, after having lived together and shared meals, would hurt deeply indeed.

Note that the Risen Jesus asked Peter, "Do you love me *more than these*?" The question was not merely, "Do you love me?" as any disciple should, but, "Do you love me more than the rest of the disciples love me?" Peter responded to Jesus not by saying, "I love you," but by saying, "Lord, you know I love you—we lived together and were the closest of friends."

Jesus gave Peter a threefold opportunity, not merely to atone for his triple denials but also to restore the special friendship they had enjoyed in Galilee. Jesus and Peter had shared many meals together; now Jesus cooked breakfast for Peter to show his love. He cooked, we can note, over a charcoal fire (John 21:9), just as Peter had denied him by a charcoal fire (John 18:18); these are the only two mentions of charcoal fires in Scripture. Peter in turn was to demonstrate his special love for Jesus by feeding his sheep—caring for Jesus' flock. Love for Jesus is expressed in service of all whom he loves.

Jesus' renewal of his friendship with Peter has implications for us. Even if we have betrayed Jesus' friendship with us, even if we have hurt him very badly, he nevertheless extends reconciliation to us. He asks us to demonstrate our love for him not merely in words but also in service.

FOR REFLECTION

How have I hurt Jesus? How did he repair our friendship and draw me back to himself? What special thing might I do now out of friendship with him?

FOUR

FOLLOWING JESUS

Follow me.

Mark 1:17

JESUS WALKS AHEAD

They were on the road, going up to Jerusalem, and Jesus was walking ahead of them; they were amazed, and those who followed were afraid. He took the twelve aside again and began to tell them what was to happen to him, saying, "See, we are going up to Jerusalem, and the Son of Man will be handed over to the chief priests and the scribes, and they will condemn him to death; then they will hand him over to the Gentiles; they will mock him, and spit upon him, and flog him, and kill him; and after three days he will rise again."

Mark 10:32–34

Mark's Gospel conveys its message through images as well as words. Here it presents the image of Jesus walking ahead of his disciples and them following after him. It is the primary image for discipleship: To be a disciple means to follow in the footsteps of Jesus.

Yet this passage from Mark paints a very sobering picture of discipleship. Those who followed after Jesus were dazed and fearful. Jesus had been telling them about his coming death (Mark 8:31; 9:31), but they did not understand what he was talking about (Mark 9:32). Peter even tried to tell Jesus that he shouldn't make such gloomy predictions (Mark 8:32).

But Jesus insisted on what he was saying: He was on his way to Jerusalem to die, and to die a particularly unpleasant death. No wonder his followers walked behind him on the road in apprehension and fear. They had no desire to watch their Lord being spat upon and mocked and tortured, even if he did promise that he would rise again.

There was probably another factor in their fear. In the passages immediately preceding and following Mark's description of Jesus walking ahead on the road to Jerusalem, the disciples expressed concern about themselves. Peter asked what they would receive, since they had given up everything to follow Jesus (Mark 10:28). Then James and John asked for favored places when Jesus came into his glory (Mark 10:35–37).

The disciples were not only fearful for what might happen to Jesus; they were also fearful about what would happen to them if Jesus met the fate that he said awaited him. And indeed, Jesus had made it clear that the path of the master had to be the path of the disciples: "If any want to become my followers, let them deny themselves and take up their cross and follow me" (Mark 8:34).

No wonder the disciples lagged behind Jesus on the road to Jerusalem: They did not like where he was leading them. And yet, despite their fears, he was leading them to resurrection. The path he was taking was the best possible path for them to walk. Even if they were filled with dread and uncertainty, they would shortly experience his triumph over death and participate in it themselves.

Jesus likewise walks ahead of us. He is the "pioneer" (Hebrews 12:2) who has blazed the path that we follow in faith.

But alas, sometimes he seems to walk too far ahead of us. We would prefer his being constantly at our side, giving us his arm to help us over obstacles on the road. We would prefer that he make more frequent rest stops to give us a chance to catch our breath.

Above all, we would prefer that he not take us along paths that lead to trials and suffering. When he allowed us to sit with him by the shore of a tranquil lake and listen to him speak to us, then our hearts burned within us at his words. Now that he walks ahead of us to Calvary, we are fearful and apprehensive.

But the important fact is that he does walk ahead of us. Our only hope for remaining in union with him is to follow after him, wherever he leads us. We cannot remain sitting by the side of the lake after he has set out for Jerusalem, or we will lose sight of him.

If we follow after him despite our uncertainty and apprehension, then where he is we shall also be (John 14:3). That is our comfort, our hope, our source of strength. No matter how dark the path of discipleship, Jesus walks ahead of us and will be awaiting us at its end. He asks us to go nowhere that he has not already gone. He asks us to endure nothing that will not lead to resurrection. He walks ahead of us and leads us along, as he led his first followers.

For Reflection

When and how did I become aware of Jesus' call to me to follow him? How do I experience his calling now?

THE NEXT STEP

*As he was setting out on a journey, a man ran
up and knelt before him, and asked him,
"Good Teacher, what must I do to inherit eternal life?" Jesus said to him,…"You know the
commandments." …He said to him, "Teacher,
I have kept all these since my youth." Jesus,
looking at him, loved him and said, "You lack
one thing; go, sell what you own, and give the
money to the poor, and you will have treasure
in heaven; then come, follow me." When he
heard this, he was shocked and went away
grieving, for he had many possessions.*

MARK 10:17–22

The encounter of the rich man and Jesus is a story we are
tempted to pass over quickly, lest we give Jesus an opening to
say to us, "You should also sell what you have and give the proceeds to the poor." We feel sorry for the well-intentioned man
from whom Jesus demanded so much, and we do not want to
find ourselves in his sandals.

Yet we cannot lightly dismiss this encounter. The man
asked, "What must I do to inherit eternal life?" and that is
inescapably a question for us as well. What must we do to be eli-
gible for union with God? Jesus looked on this man with love,
and we want Jesus to look at us with love also. It was precisely
because of Jesus' love for this man that he invited him to trade
treasure on earth for infinitely more valuable treasure in
heaven. Jesus likewise asks things of us out of his love for us.

Jesus may be inviting us to take the next step in following
him. Jesus asks different things of different people at different
times. The rich man who came to Jesus kept the commandments;

his next step involved growing in love for the poor and in detachment from possessions. But that would not have been the last thing Jesus asked of him: Following Jesus ultimately leads to Calvary, which strips away far more than possessions.

What is the next step Jesus is inviting us to take if we wish to follow him? If we are not keeping God's commandments, that is where Jesus asks us to begin. Perhaps we have an ingrained habit of sin that we have tolerated for many years; perhaps Jesus is telling us, "Now is the moment to accept the forgiveness and freedom I am offering you."

Perhaps, like the rich man, we are possessed by our possessions and need to break their grasp if we are to be free to follow Jesus and imitate his love for those in need. Perhaps, though, our next step is quite different: Jesus' invitations are specific to where we are on the path of discipleship. Jesus may be asking us to put aside something good for something better. He may be asking us to free ourselves of something that impedes our following him. He may be asking us to accept a hardship in order to more closely walk with him and serve him. It was Simon of Cyrene who most closely followed behind Jesus on the way to Calvary, and he did so only by shouldering Jesus' cross.

We may draw back from taking the next step Jesus is asking of us, as did the rich man. Or we may try and fail, perhaps repeatedly. What then?

One answer is, we don't know how the story of the rich man ultimately turned out. Perhaps his wealth progressively paled against the memory of Jesus looking at him in love; perhaps one day he was able to do what Jesus asked of him. Through God's grace there is always hope that we will be able to do what Jesus asks of us.

Jesus looks on us with love and invites us to take the next step—even if it is difficult, even if we have said no or failed many times before. It is our step toward receiving eternal life, and like eternity, it awaits us.

FOR REFLECTION

When I began to follow Jesus, what commitments or decisions did I make? How faithful have I been to living them out? What is the next step Jesus is inviting me to take in order to follow him more closely?

HAVE WE LEFT ALL?

Peter began to say to him, "Look, we have left everything and followed you."

MARK 10:28

It is not easy to leave everything in order to follow Jesus. Peter thought that he and the other disciples had left all for Jesus' sake, but the Gospels indicate that the matter was not that simple.

We usually use Peter's assertion that they had left all as the key for interpreting passages that seemingly portray the disciples abandoning their fishing businesses for Jesus: "When they had brought their boats to shore, they left everything and followed him" (Luke 5:11). But John portrays Peter and other disciples doing commercial fishing even after Jesus' Resurrection (John 21:1–14). And there always seemed to be a boat handy whenever Jesus wished to cross the Sea of Galilee. Perhaps the disciples did not leave their businesses so much as take leaves of absence to travel with Jesus. After all, most of them probably had families to support. The Gospels do not tell us enough to resolve the matter.

There are more important considerations than whether the disciples left all their possessions. The disciples did not leave all personal ambitions behind when they followed Jesus. James and John wanted Jesus to give them the two chief positions of honor and power (Mark 10:35–37), which upset the other disciples, who wanted a shot at these positions themselves (note Jesus' correction of the other disciples in Mark 10:41–45). Luke presents us with the disciples repeatedly arguing among themselves over who was greatest—even during the Last Supper (Luke 9:46; 22:24). Even their "leaving all" led to their wondering what they would thereby gain: "We have left everything and followed you. What then will we have?" (Matthew 19:27). Better for them to have left their self-seeking ambition behind rather than their nets when they set out to follow Jesus.

Nor did they leave their fears behind. They were frightened during a storm at sea with Jesus in the boat (Mark 4:36–41) and frightened a second time in a similar situation (Mark 6:50). In the moment of crisis, all of them fled, and Peter denied he even knew Jesus. After Jesus' Resurrection they hid out of fear (John 20:19), even though Mary Magdalene had told them of seeing the Risen Lord (John 20:18).

There is much else that the disciples did not leave behind when they "left all" to follow Jesus: their slowness to understand Jesus and put their absolute trust in him; their ill tempers (Luke 9:52–55); their narrowness (Mark 10:38); their reluctance to embrace the cross. But the Gospel accounts of the disciples were not written so that we could compile a catalog of their failings; they were written as examples and warnings to us, to lead us to self-examination.

Have we left all to follow Jesus?

We can perhaps look back on a moment when we made a conscious decision to give our lives to Jesus and accept him as our Lord and Savior. Or we might remember a moment when a flood of grace washed over us, and we decided to love God with our whole heart and soul and to spend our lives in his service. Such moments are important—but more important is how we live them out. We cannot answer the question "Have we left all?" simply by looking back on a decision we made; we must look at how we live each day and examine whether we have in fact left all.

We may have once decided to give ourselves completely to the Lord but, consciously or unconsciously, we may have taken back part of what we had given him. Or we may have given ourselves as completely to Jesus Christ as we were capable of doing at the moment of our decision but not touched the depths of our selves. There may be more that Jesus invites us to give him now that we were incapable of freely giving him in the past.

To leave all to follow Jesus may be like peeling an onion. We peel away all the sin and encumbrances that we can see, and we think we have gotten rid of everything—but there is another layer beneath, a layer we could not see because the first layer hid it. We cannot simply say, "I have peeled away everything for Jesus." We must instead look at ourselves anew and peel away again, as painful as that might be. To give Jesus everything is a process, not a onetime achievement.

For Reflection

What might Jesus be asking me to leave behind at this point in my life?

GIFTED FOR THE KINGDOM

Then Jesus summoned his twelve disciples and gave them authority over unclean spirits, to cast them out, and to cure every disease and every

> *sickness.... These twelve Jesus sent out with the*
> *following instructions.... "As you go, proclaim*
> *the good news, 'The kingdom of heaven has*
> *come near.' Cure the sick, raise the dead, cleanse*
> *the lepers, cast out demons. You received with-*
> *out payment; give without payment."*

MATTHEW 10:1, 5, 7–8

While the twelve were specially commissioned by Jesus, his instructions to them have meaning for all of his followers. Every Christian is called and gifted to serve God's kingdom.

Jesus chose the twelve; Jesus has likewise chosen each of us. Whether we were catching fish on the Sea of Galilee or cooking dinner or selling life insurance, one day Jesus tapped us on the shoulder and said, "Follow me."

Jesus called the twelve not only to follow him and be with him but also to share in his mission (Mark 3:14). Jesus proclaimed that the reign of God was at hand (Mark 1:15); he commissioned the twelve to proclaim the same message (Luke 9:2) and he gave this charge to his other disciples as well (Luke 10:1, 9). We, too, are to proclaim the message of Jesus. We have received the good news of salvation; we are to pass it on to others, telling them what God has done for us through Jesus.

Jesus' disciples were to carry out his works as well as proclaim his message: Jesus empowered them to heal as he healed (Luke 9:1; 10:9). The healings of Jesus were acts of mercy on the afflicted, but they were more than that. Through Jesus' healings and exorcisms, evil was vanquished and God's kingdom established (Luke 11:20). Jesus' healings were a down payment on the wholeness we will enjoy when we are fully incorporated into God's reign through resurrection; they were a foreshadowing of what will happen at the end of time (Revelation 21:3–4).

By sharing in the healing ministry of Jesus, his disciples play a role in the establishment of God's reign on earth. The final coming of God's kingdom awaits Jesus' return; in the meantime his followers are to be like that "faithful and wise slave" who diligently carried out his duties while awaiting his master's coming (Matthew 24:45–46).

But what about those of us who are not specially gifted to heal or drive out demons? Jesus' instructions to the twelve provide the answer: "You received without payment; give without payment" (Matthew 10:8). These words might also be translated, "Freely you have received; freely you are to give." The twelve were gifted to heal and exorcise, and they were to use these gifts for the sake of God's reign. Those who have been given different calls and gifts are likewise to use their gifts for the sake of the kingdom. We are all gifted (1 Corinthians 12:7) but in different ways (1 Corinthians 12:4–6). What matters is not the particular gifts we have received (that is up to God) but how we use them (that is up to us).

Give as you are gifted: Do what you are able to do to serve God and his reign. Carry out spiritual and corporal works of mercy as you are able to, work to establish justice and peace as you are able to.

Giving freely means giving in response to the generosity God has shown us. We use our gifts out of gratitude for having been gifted—above all, gifted with salvation. The standard for our giving is set by what we have received: "From everyone to whom much has been given, much will be required" (Luke 12:48).

FOR REFLECTION

How has Jesus gifted me? What has Jesus equipped me to do for the sake of God's reign?

WAITERS AND WAITRESSES

*The disciples came to him and said, "This is a
deserted place, and the hour is now late; send
the crowds away so that they may go into the
villages and buy food for themselves." Jesus
said to them, "'They need not go away; you
give them something to eat." They replied, "We
have nothing here but five loaves and two fish."*

MATTHEW 14:15–17

The disciples' suggestion made sense: The crowd had spent the
day with Jesus and were hungry, and an obvious solution was to
send them off to get something to eat. But Jesus' mission was to
gather people to himself, not scatter them; to meet their needs,
not turn them away empty. However practical the disciples'
plan might have been, it wasn't good theology.

Jesus told his disciples to give the people food, but this
struck the disciples as futile: How could they meet the needs of
the crowd with the little they had?

Jesus asked them to bring him what they had, and "taking
the five loaves and the two fish, he looked up to heaven, and
blessed and broke the loaves, and gave them to the disciples, and
the disciples gave them to the crowds" (Matthew 14:19). The disciples ended up doing what Jesus had told them to do: give food
to the crowds. As a result, "all ate and were filled" (Matthew
14:20), and there were even twelve baskets of leftovers—perhaps
a sign that the twelve were to continue to feed others.

We often focus on the miraculous character of this incident
or on its foreshadowing of the Eucharist, but there are other
dimensions worth pondering. Jesus tells his followers that we
are not to turn away the hungry, making them fend for themselves. Rather, we are to provide food to those who hunger, even

83

if we think that what we can give is inadequate. Whether it proves adequate or not is up to Jesus: The task assigned to his followers is to give what we have.

What is the food that followers of Jesus are to distribute? It can certainly include physical food. There are many exhortations in the Gospels to help the materially poor, and there is a warning that we will be judged on the basis of whether we do so or not (Matthew 25:31–46). But in Scripture, food can serve as a symbol for other nourishment, including spiritual nourishment (Matthew 4:4; John 4:34). The followers of Jesus are to distribute the food of God's Word, making available the Bread of Life (John 6:35). It is this kind of nourishing that Jesus would command of Peter: "Feed my lambs.... Tend my sheep.... Feed my sheep" (John 21:15–17).

When Jesus asks his followers to give food to others, he is asking them to become waiters and waitresses. That is how Jesus described his own role when he said, "For who is greater, the one who is at the table or the one who serves? Is it not the one at the table? But I am among you as one who serves" (Luke 22:27). The Greek word for "serve" can mean serving a meal, in the manner of Peter's mother-in-law (Mark 1:31) and Martha (Luke 10:40).

Jesus asks his followers to imitate his example, to become waiters and waitresses, to be the channels of God's love. Waiters do not grow or cook the food; they only distribute it. Waiters do not even decide what is on the menu. As God's waiters and waitresses, we simply distribute what we have been given to distribute, whether physical assistance or emotional support or spiritual nourishment—whatever matches up with the hungers of those we serve, whatever has been placed on our trays for us to carry to others.

Being a waiter or waitress was not an exalted calling in the ancient world. But it is the calling that Jesus took on himself, and it is his call to us: "You give them something to eat."

FOR REFLECTION

What is my calling? What is the particular way in which Jesus asks me to serve him?

MIGRANT WORKERS

I tell you, look around you, and see how the fields are ripe for harvesting. The reaper is already receiving wages and is gathering fruit for eternal life, so that sower and reaper may rejoice together. For here the saying holds true, "One sows and another reaps." I sent you to reap that for which you did not labor. Others have labored, and you have entered into their labor.

JOHN 4:35–38

Jesus often drew examples and comparisons from farming in his teaching because many of his listeners were farmers. Even those who did not farm for a living were intimately acquainted with farming. Commercial fishermen who fished the Sea of Galilee beached their boats within sight of cultivated fields. No one was ignorant of what it meant to sow and to reap.

Nor was anyone ignorant of the meaning of the proverb "One sows and another reaps." It was a pessimistic saying reflecting the uneven fortunes of life. A man could sow and be killed in battle before harvest or otherwise not live long enough to enjoy the fruit of his harvest (see Deuteronomy 20:6; Luke 12:16–20).

But Jesus gave this proverb a different and more positive meaning: We, as his followers, reap what others have sown. In the immediate context of John's Gospel, Jesus was referring to the harvest of converts that his disciples would reap. Saint Paul used a similar analogy when he wrote, "I planted, Apollos watered, but God gave the growth" (1 Corinthians 3:6). The harvest of the kingdom is the result of many working together as servants of God, each carrying out her or his part and benefiting from the work of others.

These words of Jesus also carry a broader meaning. Our Christian life is enriched by all those who have preceded us on the journey to our Father. We reap the benefits of their theological reflection on the mysteries of God; we reap the harvest of their evangelism; we enjoy the fruit of their labors and sacrifice. Our Christian life is a gift given to us by God, working through others as his intermediaries. There is nothing we possess that we have not been given: "What do you have that you did not receive?" (1 Corinthians 4:7).

This truth should teach us humility and gratitude. We are reaping what others have sown; we are the beneficiaries of their hard labor.

This truth also should help us keep our own labors in proper perspective. We do our share of sowing what others will reap. We will not be on this earth long enough to reap all that we have sown—either for good or for bad. If we have been the cause of scandal and loss of faith in others, we will find out the full extent of our sin only at the Last Judgment, when Jesus will confront us with the harvest that our actions have yielded. And if we have been the occasion of faith and growth in others, we likewise will not fully realize the good fruit of our efforts until that final day. If not even a cup of cold water given or withheld is to be forgotten on that day (Matthew 10:42; 25:31–46), assuredly all that we have done or failed to do for Jesus will be remembered.

While farming provides a good analogy for some important aspects of the Christian life, it is an analogy with limitations. Farmers must stay in one place, at least long enough to attempt to harvest the crop they have planted. Discipleship, on the other hand, is fittingly symbolized as a journey: It is our following after Christ, our walking in his footsteps. In our journey with him who had no place to lay his head, we are constantly on the move.

There is a way of combining the image of farming and the image of being on a journey. We might think of ourselves as migrant workers: men and women who follow after Jesus, reaping the harvests he leads us to and at the same time sowing crops for those who will come after us. What we have, we have received from those who have gone before us, sowing as they went. All that we do will result in a harvest for those who come after us— a good harvest if we sow well, a thin harvest if we do not.

Migrant workers never know how the crops they have sown turn out, for they must move on to other fields before harvesttime. Jesus' disciples must take it on faith that their service will result in good harvests for others, until that day when sower and reaper rejoice together in the presence of God and enjoy the fruit of their actions in the banquet of eternal life.

FOR REFLECTION

What are the most important things I have received from others? What am I passing on to others?

THE REBUKES OF JESUS

He turned and rebuked them.

LUKE 9:55

What does Jesus expect of us as his disciples?

The Gospels give us a wealth of his teachings and expectations, from the Sermon on the Mount (Matthew 5—7) to Jesus' Last Supper discourse (John 13—16). Meditating on these teachings and molding ourselves in accordance with them is the work of a lifetime.

The Gospels also give us some more specific clues to what Jesus expects of us, in that they describe Jesus rebuking or correcting his disciples on a number of occasions. Certainly anything Jesus had to rebuke in his first followers is something he would find equally unsatisfactory in us. By meditating on the rebukes of Jesus, we can get a clearer understanding of his expectations of us.

One series of rebukes, or corrections, had to do with the disciples' lack of faith and trust in Jesus. Jesus was disappointed that they became afraid during a storm at sea even though he was in the boat with them (Matthew 8:23–26). He chastised Peter for having such little faith after he had invited him to step out of the boat (Matthew 14:22–33). He rebuked his disciples for being faithless when they could not cure a possessed boy (Matthew 17:14–20). Even after his resurrection he had to chastise the disciples for being fearful and doubting (Luke 24:36–40; John 20:27). Jesus expects his followers to have faith-filled trust in him.

Another series of Jesus' corrections had to do with the disciples' lack of understanding. He was disappointed that they did not understand his parables (Mark 4:13) and sometimes seemed to have no more comprehension of his teachings than the crowds (Mark 7:18). He seemed exasperated when they missed the point of his words (Mark 8:14–21).

Their lack of understanding was particularly serious when it had to do with the nature of Jesus' mission and the nature of the kingdom he came to establish, and these misunderstandings earned Jesus' sternest rebukes. When Jesus taught that he would suffer and offer up his life as the Messiah and Peter rejected this, Jesus "rebuked Peter and said, 'Get behind me, Satan! For you are setting your mind not on divine things but on human things'" (Mark 8:33). When the disciples, likewise thinking that they were to be part of a kingdom of triumphant power, wanted to call down fire on an inhospitable Samaritan town, Jesus again rebuked them (Luke 9:51–56). And at the end, when they tried to prevent Jesus' arrest with the sword, Jesus had to correct them (Matthew 26:51–54).

Because the disciples had their minds set on a kingdom of this world, they consequently were concerned about who should have the most honor and power within it. Their jockeying for position earned Jesus' repeated correction. He taught them that anyone who wanted to be first must be the servant of all, just as he had come to serve and give his life as a ransom for many (Mark 9:30–37; 10:35–45). Luke presents us with the sorry picture of a dispute over who was greatest interrupting the Last Supper (Luke 22:24–27)!

The disciples earned the rebukes of Jesus on other occasions as well: He was indignant when they tried to prevent children from coming to him (Mark 10:13–16); he prevented his disciples from obstructing a man who was casting out demons in his name (Mark 9:38–40); he defended a woman who anointed him, reacting to his disciples' criticism of her act (Mark 14:3–9); he chastised his three closest friends for not keeping watch with him in Gethsemane on the night before he died (Mark 14:32–42).

All of these rebukes and corrections of Jesus should give us pause. Are we disappointing him, as his first followers did? Are we reluctant to put our full faith and trust in him? Are we slow to understand and accept his teaching? Do we secretly wish that his kingdom was one of honor and power instead of service and self-sacrifice? Are we looking out for ourselves even as we walk alongside him? Do we dispute with each other as if he were not present?

Such self-examination may prove sobering. Yet we should also keep in mind that Jesus never cut off his disciples from himself, even if he had to rebuke them. He corrected them only so that they could walk more closely with him on his way to the Father.

FOR REFLECTION

If Jesus were to speak a word of correction to me, what might he say?

FOLLOWING JESUS

When the days drew near for him to be taken up, he set his face to go to Jerusalem.

LUKE 9:51

Most of us dislike change—especially change that is forced upon us. Our jobs might not be perfect, but it is very unsettling when our company goes out of business and we have to find new work. Moving to another city is a difficult disruption for many families. The death of a spouse or parent or child is a heavy blow, and our loved one's absence leaves a lingering emptiness. The list of painful changes goes on and on: loss of health, the limitations inherent in aging, old forms of prayer no longer seeming to work, upheaval in our parish.

Luke constructed his Gospel with a major pivot point. Verse 51 of chapter 9 marks the beginning of Jesus' journey to Jerusalem. Until this point Jesus' ministry was centered in Galilee. All of his followers were apparently Galileans (Luke 22:59; 23:55; Acts 1:11). No mention is made in Luke's Gospel of Jesus having been back to Jerusalem after he was twelve years old.

Luke therefore portrays the journey to Jerusalem as a turning point in Jesus' public ministry. It is not only a change in geography but a change in the shape of Jesus' ministry. Put bluntly, Jesus went to Jerusalem to die: "When the days drew near for him to be taken up, he set his face to go to Jerusalem."

Just before setting out on the journey to Jerusalem, Jesus told his followers what lay ahead: "The Son of Man must undergo great suffering, and be rejected…and be killed, and on the third day be raised" (Luke 9:22). Jesus had no suicidal tendencies, but he knew the inevitable outcome of remaining faithful to his Father's will for him. His followers, on the other hand, were slow to understand, even when he repeatedly told them where the journey would end: "But they did not understand this saying; its meaning was concealed from them, so that they could not perceive. And they were afraid to ask him about this saying" (Luke 9:45).

We who have trouble accepting change can empathize with these first disciples. What trauma could be greater than having the one they followed as the Messiah face execution? What greater change could there be than from the Mount of Transfiguration (Luke 9:28–36) to the hill of Calvary? And what greater demand could face them than Jesus' invitation to follow in his footsteps and lose their lives for his sake (Luke 9:23–24)?

It is no wonder then that they reacted to Jesus' words with fear and confusion and followed in a daze: "They were on the road, going up to Jerusalem, and Jesus was walking ahead of them; they were amazed, and those who followed were afraid" (Mark 10:32).

What might this journey of Jesus and his disciples to Jerusalem mean to us as his followers today? I believe it is a warning that we cannot count on remaining forever in the familiar Galilean villages of our lives and certainly not on the Mount of Transfiguration. There may come a point when the Jesus we follow sets out for Jerusalem, and to be with him we must go there too. We may have to kneel beside him in Gethsemane and join with him in praying, "Not my will but yours be done" (Luke 22:42).

Luke devotes a significant portion of his Gospel to Jesus' journey to Jerusalem: Jesus sets out for Jerusalem at Luke 9:51 and the first mention of his being in the city is made in Luke 21:37. By making a journey the setting of so much of his Gospel, Luke conveys that the Christian life is a journey. Being a follower of Jesus is not a static state but a process, not an achievement but growth. We are always in transition, leaving some things behind, striving for others.

Change is inherent in following Jesus: Following implies that someone is walking ahead of us, leading us, showing us the way. We cannot sit still and follow. We must rise and step forth, confident in Jesus, who walks ahead of us, confident that he will keep us on the right path.

FOR REFLECTION

Is my life now in transition? What transitions lie ahead for me? How can I use them to grow in my relationship with Jesus?

FEED MY SHEEP

"Do you love me?… Feed my sheep. Very truly, I tell you, when you were younger, you used to fasten your own belt and to go wherever you wished. But when you grow old, you will stretch out your hands, and someone else will fasten a belt around you and take you where you do not wish to go." (He said this to indicate

the kind of death by which he would glorify
God.) After this he said to him, "Follow me."

JOHN 21:17–19

Jesus' last invitation to Peter echoed his first: "Follow me" (Mark 1:16–18). The last invitation was charged with more meaning than the first, for much had happened in between—particularly the crucifixion and resurrection of Jesus. When Peter first began following Jesus, he was following him into the unknown. This last invitation was an invitation to the cross.

Jesus apparently was quoting a popular proverb observing that, while the young can dress themselves and go about as they want, the elderly may be dependent on others for help in getting dressed and going places. Jesus gave this proverb a deeper meaning, making it an allusion to the kind of death Peter would suffer. Peter's arms would be stretched out and tied to the crossbeam of a cross, and Peter would be led away to be crucified.

John's Gospel calls Peter's death the means by which he would glorify God. Jesus used similar language for his own crucifixion: It was his hour of glorification (John 12:23–24). In the context of speaking about his death, Jesus proclaimed, "Whoever serves me must follow me" (John 12:26). When Jesus asked Peter to serve him (to feed his sheep) and to follow him, he was inviting Peter to the cross. Peter's service as the shepherd of Jesus' flock would result in his crucifixion in Rome during Nero's persecution.

What about we who will not glorify God by suffering death as a martyr? What meaning do Jesus' words to Peter have for us?

On the human level some of us may experience the truth of the proverb Jesus quoted. We will get old and may need help getting dressed; we may find ourselves in a nursing home when we would rather be living in our own house or apartment. It will be a time when our only recourse will be to embrace the mystery of the cross and believe that following Jesus leads to eternal life, even if our following is now but a slow shuffle.

If we are blessed with good health to the end of our lives, Jesus' words still carry meaning for us. Jesus asked Peter to serve him by feeding his sheep; Jesus likewise asks us to serve him, and he has given each of us a particular way of doing so. There are all kinds of sheep and all kinds of hunger; there are all sorts of ways in which we may feed them. Jesus talked about our abilities to serve in his parable of the talents (Matthew 25:14–30); we will be judged on the basis of our use of our talents to help others (Matthew 25:31–46).

To persevere in our service of Jesus, in our use of our talents and gifts and opportunities, can mean following Jesus along the way of the cross. When we were young we might have had many choices, but we committed ourselves to a certain path or a particular form of service. Now it may be old hat for us or even a little stale and confining. Yet we realize that the way in which we are able to glorify God is through remaining faithful to our service, even bound to our service as Peter would be bound to the cross, for the sheep we are feeding are still hungry.

Jesus asks us, "Do you love me?" He invites us, "Feed my sheep" and "Follow me."

FOR REFLECTION

Have I grown weary of following Jesus? What might I do to rekindle my zeal?

FIVE

TO PRAY
AS JESUS

Lord, teach us to pray.

LUKE 11:1

WHY WE PRAY

When you are praying, do not heap up empty phrases as the Gentiles do; for they think that they will be heard because of their many words. Do not be like them, for your Father knows what you need before you ask him. Pray then in this way:
Our Father in heaven,
  hallowed be your name.
  Your kingdom come.
  Your will be done,
      on earth as it is in heaven.
  Give us this day our daily bread.
  And forgive us our debts,
      as we also have forgiven our debtors.
  And do not bring us to the time of trial,
      but rescue us from the evil one.

MATTHEW 6:7–13

If our heavenly Father knows what we need before we ask, why do we need to ask at all?

It is certainly not to nag God into doing what he is reluctant to do, nor is it to earn the favors he gives us: Jesus would say that pagans might understand prayer in such terms, but not those who have grasped what he has taught about his Father. His Father knows the things we need and will provide for us (Matthew 6:25–31). His Father even provides for those who do not deserve or acknowledge his care (Matthew 5:44–45). He is not a God who has to be talked into loving us.

What then does our prayer accomplish? Let us look at the prayer Jesus taught us and examine what we are asking when we offer this prayer. If this is the way Jesus taught us to pray, then it must accomplish what our prayer is meant to accomplish.

The first three petitions of the Lord's Prayer are closely related. They ask God to manifest his holiness, to establish his kingdom, to accomplish his will on earth. In praying these petitions we are primarily asking God to act, rather than praying that men and women will hallow God's name, bring about his kingdom and do his will (although these are certainly good things to ask for in prayer). The accent in these petitions as they are phrased in the Greek text of Matthew's Gospel is on God acting. We are asking in three slightly different ways for God to complete his plan of salvation for the world.

The remaining petitions of the Lord's Prayer also have something in common: They focus on our basic individual needs. We need bread and the necessities of life each day; we need forgiveness for our sins; we need security in times of testing and protection from evil. These are our basic needs for staying alive physically and spiritually, and we turn to God as the one who is not only able to satisfy them but also, as Jesus teaches, eager to do so (Matthew 7:7–11).

But again, doesn't God know what our needs are before we ask? Doesn't he know that we stand in need of daily sustenance and forgiveness and protection? So what is the point of asking? Likewise, what is the point of asking God to complete his plan of salvation for the world? Isn't that something that God is determined to do, even apart from our asking?

We ask not because God is prone to forget what needs doing but because we are prone to forget the most important truths about the meaning of life on earth. We are all too easily caught up in the passing concerns of each day. We need regularly to remind ourselves that we are a part of God's plan to establish his reign, reconciling everything to himself through Jesus Christ.

If we all too easily forget the big picture, we also all too easily overlook what our basic needs really are. Our prayers of petition can become a wish list of niceties instead of focusing on what is truly important for our welfare, now and eternally. The prayer Jesus taught us draws our attention back to our basic necessities.

In praying the prayer that Jesus taught us, we acknowledge our dependence on God to do what only God can do: complete his plan of salvation and preserve us as a part of it. We express our needs to God because he alone can and does satisfy them. The prayer aligns us with what God is doing. Jesus told his disciples, "Strive first for the kingdom of God and his righteousness, and all these things will be given to you as well" (Matthew 6:33). Praying the prayer Jesus taught us is our way of saying, "Yes! Let all you do come to pass!"

FOR REFLECTION

How often do I pray? How do I pray? What do I pray for?

DAILY BREAD

Meanwhile the disciples were urging him,
"Rabbi, eat something." But he said to them,
"I have food to eat that you do not know about."
So the disciples said to one another, "Surely no
one has brought him something to eat?" Jesus
said to them, "My food is to do the will of him
who sent me and to complete his work."

JOHN 4:31–34

The petition we make in the Our Father, "Give us this day our daily bread," seems straightforward in English, but it is less so in the Greek text of the New Testament. The problem lies in a peculiar Greek word. *Epiousion* is used by both Matthew (6:11) and Luke (11:3) to characterize the bread for which we are praying: "Give us this day our *epiousion* bread." This word is found nowhere else in the Bible, nor anywhere in all of Greek literature. Consequently, there is great uncertainty over what this rare word means.

Various ancient and modern scholars have suggested that *epiousion* might perhaps mean "for tomorrow," or perhaps "for today" or perhaps even "necessary for existence." Saint Jerome, who translated the Bible into Latin, knew of the "for tomorrow" interpretation, but he translated *epiousion* into Latin either as "daily" or as *supersubstantialis*—often understood as a reference to the Eucharist.

We cannot know for certain what Matthew and Luke had in mind when they wrote *epiousion*, nor is there any way to recover the earlier Aramaic word used by Jesus when he taught the Our Father. There is therefore no reason why we should not continue to pray the Our Father as we have learned it, asking for "daily bread." On the other hand, the obscurity of this petition in the Greek New Testament can lead us to reflect on what we mean when we pray for "daily bread" and perhaps to personalize this petition in our prayer.

The word *bread* in Scripture can carry the broader meaning of food in general, since bread was the basic food of ordinary people in biblical times and provided a substantial part of their daily intake of calories. Many people in today's world pray for their daily bread or subsistence when they get up in the morning, because having enough to eat that day is far from certain. Most of us, however, have an ample supply of groceries on hand; for us to ask for our "daily bread" can be to acknowledge that our food and life come from God.

But food can also carry a broader meaning, as in Jesus' words, "My food is to do the will of him who sent me and to complete his work." In praying for our daily bread, we can therefore be asking for the food of doing God's will that day, for the gift of being able to serve God, for the blessing of seeing value in our work.

This is not a gift to be taken for granted. Many people set about the duties of the day with little more than a numb "I gotta do this." Many have trouble seeing that what they do makes any difference for the coming of God's kingdom on earth. Most have to care for families, punch time clocks, carry out mundane obligations. In such situations, what does it mean to ask for the daily bread of serving God?

No matter what our circumstances, we can pray that we will be God's servant in those circumstances. We might not expect to do anything different that day, but we can ask for the grace to do it well and the grace to recognize that what we do is God's will for us. We can also pray that God will give us special openings to serve him, perhaps in the people we meet that day, perhaps through unexpected opportunities.

"Give us this day our daily bread"—the bread of serving God, the bread of seeing our day through his eyes, the bread of imitating Jesus, whose food was to do the will of his Father and complete his work. That is indeed food that satisfies our hunger and sustains us.

What do I have in mind when I pray, "Give us this day our daily bread"? What are my greatest daily needs?

LORD, HAVE MERCY!

> *There were two blind men sitting by the road-side. When they heard that Jesus was passing by, they shouted, "Lord, have mercy on us, Son of David!" The crowd sternly ordered them to be quiet; but they shouted even more loudly, "Have mercy on us, Lord, Son of David!" Jesus stood still and called them, saying, "What do you want me to do for you?" They said to him, "Lord, let our eyes be opened." Moved with compassion, Jesus touched their eyes. Immediately they regained their sight and followed him.*

MATTHEW 20:30–34

Catholics of my generation remember reciting the *Kyrie eleison* at every Mass, a prayer that we now pray in English as "Lord, have mercy." Although the rest of the Mass was in Latin, *Kyrie eleison* are Greek words. It would be up to those who study the history of the liturgy to explain why this prayer was preserved in Greek, but one factor might be that the words *Kyrie eleison* appear several times in the Greek text of the Gospel of Matthew, on the lips of those who are imploring Jesus for help. Those who came to Jesus spoke to him in their common language of Aramaic, but Matthew translated their words into the petition *Kyrie eleison*, "Lord, have mercy."

We first hear these words spoken by the Canaanite woman whose daughter was tormented by a demon. Even though she was not Jewish, she cried out to Jesus, "Have mercy on me, Lord" (Matthew 15:22). She persisted in her plea for mercy, eager for the crumbs that would fall from the table of Jesus, until her daughter was healed.

Likewise, the man whose son was possessed by an evil spirit that threw him into the fire cried out to Jesus, "*Kyrie eleison*," "Lord, have mercy on my son" (Matthew 17:15). The disciples had been unable to heal his son, and he turned to Jesus. Mark records the man's anguished cry, "I believe; help my unbelief" (Mark 9:24). I want to believe in you and try to believe in you; have mercy on my weak faith and have mercy on my son. Jesus did have mercy on them.

The two blind men sitting by the road outside Jericho also cried out, "*Kyrie eleison*" (Matthew 20:30), shouting to make themselves heard above the crowd, persisting in their plea for pity even when others tried to hush them. Their cry was heard by Jesus; he healed them, and they began to follow him as his disciples. Matthew presents them to us as models of discipleship: Jesus touches and restores us; we respond by following him.

In all of these instances, *Kyrie eleison* was not a prayer that people recited unthinkingly and mechanically but a cry that came from their hearts, a cry of desperate need and dependence on Jesus. Lord, have mercy, because my daughter is tormented by demons. Lord, have mercy, because we are blind and doomed to a life of begging unless you hear our cry and heal us. Lord, have mercy, for we desperately need your mercy.

We, however, find it all too easy to recite the words "Lord, have mercy" at Mass without thinking too much about what we are asking for. The familiar pattern of the liturgy carries us along, whether we are conscious or not of needing the mercy of Jesus. But we desperately do need it: not perhaps at the moment for physical healing but certainly for healing from sin and ultimately from death.

Healing from sin is the context in which we pray, "Lord, have mercy," at Mass, as a part of the Penitential Rite. Our prayer is a cry for forgiveness; our plea is that Jesus would take pity on us in our sinfulness. If we were to truly acknowledge our spiritual state, our cry to him would be even more heartfelt than the cry of the Canaanite woman or the Jewish father or the two blind men.

And as in the case of the two blind men, the mercy Jesus extends to us is meant to result in our changed lives. We cannot pray for mercy without being willing to extend mercy to others. That is the point of Jesus' parable about the two debtors (Matthew 18:23–35). Matthew used forms of the Greek word *eleison* in presenting Jesus' teaching: "Should you not have *had mercy* on your fellow slave, as I *had mercy* on you?" (Matthew 18:33; italics added).

The mercy we ask for is the mercy we must give. Lord, have mercy—and make us merciful.

FOR REFLECTION

How am I most in need of God's mercy right now? How confidently can I ask God to have mercy on me?

INTERCESSORY PRAYER

"Simon, Simon, listen! Satan has demanded
to sift all of you like wheat, but I have prayed
for you that your own faith may not fail; and

> *you, when once you have turned back,*
> *strengthen your brothers." And he said to him,*
> *"Lord, I am ready to go with you to prison and*
> *to death!" Jesus said, "I tell you, Peter, the cock*
> *will not crow this day, until you have denied*
> *three times that you know me."*

LUKE 22:31–34

There is a mystery to intercessory prayer. How can our words, our yearnings of heart, our sacrifices, make a difference in what God does or in what happens to another person? How can our prayers change what God has eternally foreseen?

Some may doubt that prayer makes any difference. Sometimes their skepticism stems from their own apparently unanswered prayer: "I prayed for my son, but he still left the church." "I prayed for my husband to get well, but he died."

But others can attest to their prayers being answered, their intercessions being heard. They may not be able to explain how their prayers could make a difference with God or why some prayers seem to go unanswered, but they know from experience that God does hear and answer prayer.

The mystery of intercessory prayer is most apparent when our prayers are the most fervent and spring from our deepest love. We pray for people we dearly love, interceding for their well-being and health, interceding even for their relationship with God. But as we pray we are aware that God loves them with a far deeper love than we could humanly have for them. Our words may be little more than reminding God of how much he loves them.

Can our prayers increase God's love by one iota? Is there any need for God's love to be increased, since his love is perfect? We don't have answers to our questions, but we continue praying nonetheless, out of our love for the one we are praying for. We trust the instincts of our hearts more than our fuzzy thinking.

A basic principle of the Christian life is, when in doubt, look to what Jesus did in a similar situation, and imitate that. The Gospels present us with at least one clear case of Jesus' intercessory prayer for another person. During the Last Supper Jesus told Peter that he had prayed for him, that his faith might not fail. There are several striking lessons in Jesus' doing so.

First, Jesus recognized Peter as one specially favored by his Father. When Peter acknowledged Jesus to be the Messiah and Son of God, Jesus responded, "Blessed are you, Simon son of Jonah! For flesh and blood has not revealed this to you, but my Father in heaven" (Matthew 16:17). Yet Jesus prayed for Peter: God's love for someone, or even God's special favor for someone, does not make our prayers for that person superfluous.

Second, Jesus prayed for Peter, asking that God strengthen his faith so that it would not fail, even though he knew that Peter's faith would falter and that he would deny him three times before the next cockcrow (Luke 22:34). Jesus prayed a prayer that he knew would not be completely answered! And in light of its not being completely answered, Jesus went on to pray that Peter would strengthen the other disciples "once you have turned back"—turned back to Jesus. His prayer seems to be a prayer that Peter's fall would not utterly destroy his faith and that Peter would recover from it and be able to carry on his leadership role among the disciples. The second part of Jesus' prayer was fully answered; Peter wept bitterly over his cowardly denials (Luke 22:62) and resumed his role as leader.

Yet how could Jesus pray for something and his prayer not be completely answered? If there is a mystery to our intercessory prayer, there is a far greater mystery in the intercessory prayer of Jesus.

Third, the most simple and certain lesson from this passage is the need for and legitimacy of intercessory prayer. Whatever mysteries there may be about Jesus' prayer, Jesus prayed for Peter. Whatever mysteries there may be to our own intercessory prayer, we are on solid ground in imitating the example of Jesus. We too are to pray for those we love.

FOR REFLECTION

Who are the people I pray for most often? How faithful am I in praying for them?

CONFIDENCE IN PRAYER

Suppose one of you has a friend, and you go to him at midnight and say to him, "Friend, lend me three loaves of bread; for a friend of mine has arrived, and I have nothing to set before him." And he answers from within, "Do not bother me; the door has already been locked, and my children are with me in bed; I cannot get up and give you anything." I tell you, even though he will not get up and give him anything because he is his friend, at least because of his persistence he will get up and give him whatever he needs.

LUKE 11:5–8

Jesus based his parables on the life experiences of his listeners. Because our culture is different from the culture in which Jesus lived, we sometimes have to make mental adjustments as we read the parables.

Have any of us ever been awakened at midnight by a friend wanting three loaves of bread? Probably not. Were we, we might tell him that that is what convenience stores are for.

But there were no twenty-four–hour convenience stores in the time of Jesus. Each family baked its own bread, usually a day's supply at a time. A family who had run out of bread might know a neighbor who had some left over.

There were no hotel chains either, and travelers normally stayed with friends or relatives. Even when guests arrived unexpectedly, hospitality was an almost sacred duty. One might even have to wake up a friend to help out.

One might even have to wake up a friend's whole family, since the houses of ordinary people often were just single rooms, used for shelter from the weather and for sleeping. A man was asleep on a mat on the floor, his family sleeping around him, when a friend awakened him to ask for bread. Jesus asked his listeners to imagine the man's response to such a request.

In the culture of Jesus' time, the man would, of course, get up and give bread to his friend, even though it meant waking his family. To turn down a request to help a guest would have been shameful, for the duty of hospitality fell on the whole village. The family could get back to sleep again, but to refuse bread for a guest would bring dishonor in a culture that prized honor.

We often miss this implication of the parable because a key word in verse 8 is translated as "persistence"—the persistence of the friend asking for bread. But Kenneth Bailey, a scholar who studied the parables against the backdrop of Middle Eastern village life, notes that the Greek word translated as "persistence" literally means "shamelessness."[1] Furthermore, this "shamelessness" refers not to the friend asking for bread but to the man who was awakened, and it has the sense of avoiding shameful conduct. The parable does not have to do with persistence in asking but with a request being granted because turning it down would be dishonorable.

Jesus told this as a parable about prayer. It has been understood to teach the importance of persistence in prayer, much as does the parable of the corrupt judge and the persistent widow (Luke 18:1–8). But Bailey suggests a different interpretation. Jesus' first listeners would have found it unthinkable that anyone would turn down a request, even if inconvenient, for bread for a guest. If such a request was not granted out of friendship, it certainly would be granted to avoid the loss of honor that denying it would entail. And if one could be confident of a friend's meeting one's needs for the sake of honor, how much more confident can one be when approaching God?

In favor of this interpretation are the words of Jesus four verses later, which draw a similar lesson: "If you, then, who are evil, know how to give good gifts to your children, how much more will the heavenly Father give the Holy Spirit to those who ask him!" (Luke 11:13). We can pray with great confidence, for God is far more responsive to us than we are to our friends and children.

FOR REFLECTION

How confident am I that God hears my prayers? That he answers my prayers?

ABBA, FATHER

He took with him Peter and James and John, and began to be distressed and agitated. And he said to them, "I am deeply grieved, even to death; remain here, and keep awake." And

> *going a little farther, he threw himself on the*
> *ground and prayed that, if it were possible, the*
> *hour might pass from him. He said, "Abba,*
> *Father, for you all things are possible; remove*
> *this cup from me; yet, not what I want, but*
> *what you want."*

MARK 14:33–36

Jesus taught us to pray to our heavenly Father with confidence and even intimacy. He knows our needs before we ask (Matthew 6:8); he loves us far more than we love our own children (Luke 11:13). Jesus authorized us to approach his Father as our Father, crying out "Abba, Father" (Romans 8:15–17; Galatians 4:6).

But what about those times when God seems distant or absent from our lives? When everything seems to be going wrong, and we have a hard time stirring up any conviction that God cares for us? When words of prayer stick dry in our throats?

Not every Christian may experience such times, but a good many do. The causes can vary. Physical and emotional fatigue can numb us; bouts of depression can send us careening toward despair; illness may sap our spiritual as well as physical strength; our sins take their toll. And beyond these causes there may be God's pruning action, drawing us closer to him by stripping away our false notions of him and our false motives in serving him.

Whatever the causes might be, the end results may be the same—we lack a sense of intimacy with God; we have little conviction that he is caring for us; we find it very difficult to pray. We may know that our feelings are an unreliable guide in spiritual matters. We may know that God loves us no matter how we feel and cares for us no matter the mess we are in. But what we know in our head has a hard time making it into our hearts and onto our tongues; our prayer remains barren.

Jesus gave us an example of how we should pray when we find ourselves in such a state. He taught by example even when it came to anguished prayer.

Consider what was on Jesus' mind the night before he died. He knew that suffering and death awaited him. He knew that his closest friends would betray, deny, abandon him. He experienced the same turmoil of emotions that we would in such circumstances. He was "distressed and agitated"; he was "deeply grieved, even to death" (Mark 14:33–34). "In his anguish he prayed more earnestly, and his sweat became like great drops of blood falling down on the ground" (Luke 22:44).

On previous occasions Jesus' prayers had been answered with reassuring words from heaven (Luke 3:21–22; 9:28–35). But in his hour of anguish, no voice proclaimed, "You are my Son, the Beloved; with you I am well pleased" (Mark 1:11). There was only silence and darkness and the snores of friends.

How could Jesus have confidence in a God who would let him suffer and die? How could Jesus pray with intimacy to a God who made no response? What words of prayer could be used in a time of such great distress?

Jesus used the words "Abba, Father,…not what I want, but what you want" (Mark 14:36). Even in his hour of greatest anguish, Jesus called upon God as his Abba, his loving Father. Even when faced with suffering and death, Jesus entrusted himself to his Father's will.

And that is how he taught us to pray, no matter how we feel, no matter what the circumstances. "Pray then in this way: Our Father in heaven…. Your will be done" (Matthew 6:9–10). Even when we least feel like it, we are to pray to God as our loving Father and trust his will for us. That is how Jesus prayed in an hour of his darkness. That is how we are to pray, no matter the darkness.

In my private prayers how do I address God: As God? Father? Lord? By another name? What does the way I address God reveal about my relationship with him?

CLOSE TO GOD

Jesus took with him Peter and John and James,
and went up on the mountain to pray. And
while he was praying, the appearance of his face
changed, and his clothes became dazzling white.

LUKE 9:28–29

They went to a place called Gethsemane; and
he said to his disciples, "Sit here while I pray."
He took with him Peter and James and John,
and began to be distressed and agitated.

MARK 14:32–33

It would be difficult to juxtapose two scenes from the life of Jesus that are in more apparent contrast than his Transfiguration and his agony in the garden.

Jesus' Transfiguration is the preeminent biblical example of a "mountaintop" experience: His appearance became radiant while he was praying (Luke 9:29), and he heard God commend him as his beloved Son (Mark 9:7). Peter was so filled with joy that he suggested putting up tents so that they could stay there longer.

Jesus' agony in the garden was seemingly quite opposite. Jesus was distressed and agitated, "deeply grieved, even to death" (Mark 14:34). "In his anguish he prayed more earnestly, and his sweat became like great drops of blood falling down on the ground" (Luke 22:44). Peter made no suggestion that tents be erected to prolong this scene.

We must wonder how Jesus could have such completely different experiences in prayer. Surely, we might think, anyone who has had an experience like the Transfiguration should be forever immune to the kind of agonized prayer Jesus experienced in Gethsemane. It is hard for us to even keep these two scenes in our minds at once.

Yet there is good evidence that that is precisely what we are intended to do. There are too many parallels between the Transfiguration and the agony in the garden for these similarities to be accidental. They demand being understood together.

The setting of both was a mountain (Luke 9:28; 22:39). In both incidents Jesus went there to pray. The Father of Jesus figured importantly in both scenes: as the one who acknowledged Jesus as his beloved Son during the Transfiguration (Mark 9:7) and as the one to whom Jesus called out as his "Abba, Father" during his agony (Mark 14:36).

Both events speak a powerful word to us about what it meant for Jesus to be the Son of God, fully human and fully divine. Both therefore also speak to us about what it means to imitate Christ and be joined to him. The Transfiguration was an anticipation of the glory of the Risen Christ, a glory we hope to share when we join him in resurrection. In his agony in the garden, he embraced the way of his Father, which led to resurrection, a way we must also embrace.

Both moments give us a privileged glimpse of Jesus' intimate relationship with his Father. We might think that Jesus was much closer to his Father on the mountain of Transfiguration than during his agony in the garden. But that is to take too psychological a view of these two events. In both moments Jesus was totally submissive to his Father's will. In both moments his Father looked upon him as his Beloved Son.

It is easy to embrace God in a moment of glory; it is much more difficult to do so in a time of anguish. Yet we may be nearer to God in our moments of anguish than in our times of consolation. Perhaps geography itself bears witness to this, the kind of hint that the fathers of the church delighted in exploring. The traditional site of Jesus' Transfiguration is Mount Tabor in Galilee; the traditional location of Gethsemane is an olive grove near the foot of the Mount of Olives, in the Kidron Valley. Mount Tabor rises 1,850 feet above sea level. But because Jerusalem lies in the hill country, the Garden of Gethsemane, even though it is in a valley, is about twenty-two hundred feet above sea level. So the valley of the agony is nearer the heavens than the peak of Transfiguration. And we can note that Calvary has a higher elevation than either of them.

Are we as near to God during our moments of anguished prayer as we are during our mountaintop experiences? Are we even closer to him when we cry out in pain, "Abba, thy will be done," than when we are flooded with grace and all is easy? The answer rises above Calvary, and it is a cross.

FOR REFLECTION

When is it easiest for me to say to God, your will be done? In what circumstance do I find it the most difficult? What was the outcome when I last told God, your will be done?

SIX

LIVING AS JESUS' DISCIPLES

For I have set you an example, that you also should do as I have done to you.

JOHN 13:15

STRIVING FOR GOD'S REIGN

Therefore do not worry, saying, "What will we eat?" or "What will we drink?" or "What will we wear?" For it is the Gentiles who strive for all these things; and indeed your heavenly Father knows that you need all these things. But strive first for the kingdom of God and his righteousness, and all these things will be given to you as well.

MATTHEW 6:31–33

Jesus did not deny that we need food and clothing, but he said that satisfying our material needs should not be the number one priority in our lives. Our first priority should be to strive for God's kingdom and God's righteousness.

What does it mean to strive for God's kingdom and righteousness?

Jesus came to proclaim and inaugurate God's kingdom or reign. "The time is fulfilled, and the kingdom of God has come near," he announced, "repent, and believe in the good news" (Mark 1:15). Jesus established God's reign on earth by his teaching and healing and exorcisms (Luke 11:20); through him the kingdom of God became present in our midst (Luke 17:21). Striving for the kingdom of God first of all means accepting the good news that God's reign is being established through Jesus.

Yet there is still need for us to pray, "Thy kingdom come." God's reign is not yet completely established "on earth as it is in heaven." That will only happen when Jesus returns and brings all to fulfillment. We must seek to live under the reign of God here and now, but we also must wait and pray for God to finish what he began through Jesus. That too is part of our striving for or seeking the kingdom of God.

When Jesus tells us to strive for "God's righteousness," we might think he is asking us to live righteous and just lives, but that is not the primary meaning. "God's righteousness" is first of all the righteousness God bestows on us: Another word for it would be salvation. Paul speaks of not having any righteousness on his own; his righteousness comes from God through faith in Christ (Philippians 3:9). So too we seek to be made upright by God, receiving salvation through Jesus Christ. That is the righteousness that we are to "hunger and thirst for" (Matthew 5:6). The righteousness God bestows enables us to live upright lives; the mercy God shows enables us to be merciful.

Striving for God's kingdom and for God's righteousness, then, both first of all mean looking to God for what only he can accomplish. Only God can establish his reign; only God can make us righteous. Seeking first God's reign and righteousness means making God's actions our number one concern. It means shifting our perspective from what we do to what God does. In terms of material concerns—what we are to eat and wear, how we are to pay our bills—it means shifting our focus from our needs and desires to God's plans for us.

While the accent must be on what God does, our response is essential. God gives us the grace to live upright lives so that we will in fact live uprightly; Jesus inaugurated God's reign on earth so that we would be a part of it. Jesus' teachings spell out what it means to behave as someone living under God's reign (review the Sermon on the Mount, for example, Matthew's 5—7).

It takes trust to not worry about what we eat and wear and how our bills will get paid and instead make God's reign and righteousness our priority, trusting that God will care for us. But it also requires shifting our perspective from material needs to more important matters and from what we do to what God does. For some of us this is a shift that takes a lifetime to accomplish. Perhaps that is why Jesus phrased his command in terms of striving. Fortunately, our Father in heaven knows all our needs—even our need for greater trust in him—and stands ready to meet them.

FOR REFLECTION

What are my goals in life? If how I use my free time is an indication, what are my highest priorities?

DAILY CROSS, DAILY BREAD

Then he said to them all, "If any want to become my followers, let them deny themselves and take up their cross daily and follow me."

LUKE 9:23

He said to them, "When you pray, say:
Father, hallowed be your name.
Your kingdom come.
Give us each day our daily bread."

LUKE 11:2–3

Translations of Luke's Gospel have Jesus twice using the word *daily* in special instructions to his disciples. We must take up our crosses daily if we are to follow him; we are to pray that our Father will give us each day our daily bread. Is there any connection between these two daily dimensions of discipleship?

All of us have our own particular crosses: chronic sickness or infirmity, financial hardships, the struggle to overcome addictions or depression—the list goes on and includes whatever burdens make our shoulders ache with fatigue.

We cannot rid ourselves of these crosses with a snap of our fingers, and so we must follow Jesus, bearing their weight. This means not losing faith, not giving up hope, not letting our charity grow cold, despite the burdens we bear. Even if we fall beneath the weight of these crosses, we must get up again and stagger after Jesus.

What does it mean to pray for daily bread? Since bread was the staple food in the biblical world, bread symbolized all food, all sustenance. To pray for daily bread means more than praying for two slices of Wonder Bread for our luncheon sandwich. "Give us each day our daily bread" means give us each day all that we need to sustain us for this day.

One of our daily needs is the particular strength to bear our daily crosses. For the infirm it is the strength to bear the pain and debility of the infirmity that day. For an alcoholic it is the grace not to drink that day. For whatever weighs us down, it is the strength to follow Jesus with that burden, trusting in him, clinging to him that day. That is the daily bread we ask from our Father.

While many crosses are involuntary, there are also crosses that we can choose to shoulder or not. A good deal of Christian service falls into this category. We can use the gifts that God has given us as he would have us use them, or we can pretend that we are ungifted. We can turn away from the needs of others, or we can try to help meet their needs, usually at some cost to us. We can take the burdens of others on our shoulders, or we can stand idly by, merely feeling sorry that they suffer.

"Give us each day our daily bread" can therefore be a prayer for the grace to persevere in using our gifts of service, no matter how bored or fatigued we have become. It can be a prayer that God will sustain us that day as caregivers and comforters. It can be a prayer for the strength and love to bear the burdens of others, shifting some of the weight from their shoulders to ours.

"Give us each day our daily bread" can even mean "Give me today the bread of bearing another's cross." Why would we ever want to pray for a cross? Simply because Jesus does not invite us to follow him empty-shouldered. There are plenty of crosses in this world, more than enough to go around. Jesus went to his Father bearing a cross, and he asks those who would follow him to do the same.

For Reflection

What particular burdens and crosses is Jesus asking me to bear? How willingly do I shoulder them?

SIMON OF CYRENE

Then they led him out to crucify him. They
compelled a passer-by, who was coming
in from the country, to carry his cross; it
was Simon of Cyrene, the father of Alexander
and Rufus.

MARK 15:20–21

Power has its privileges, and one of the privileges that Roman soldiers enjoyed in the lands in which they were stationed was the right to press local civilians into service. A Roman soldier could tap someone's shoulder with the flat of his spear, and that person would be obliged to carry the soldier's baggage or other burdens for up to one mile.

Jesus had this practice in mind when he taught his followers, "If anyone forces you to go one mile, go also the second mile" (Matthew 5:41). Jews resented being treated like pack animals by Roman soldiers, so Jesus' command probably shocked the disciples. Yet this teaching of Jesus is no more shocking than some of his other commands—to love our enemies, for example (Matthew 5:43–48).

One of those who was pressed into service by Roman soldiers was a certain Simon from Cyrene. Cyrene was a city on the north coast of Africa, in what is present-day Libya, with a sizable Jewish population. Simon either had moved from Cyrene to Jerusalem (perhaps owning land there) or had come to Jerusalem to celebrate the Feast of the Passover. In any case, he was passing by when Roman soldiers needed someone to carry Jesus' cross, and they picked him. Their choice was apparently arbitrary; there is no indication that Simon was a disciple of Jesus.

Yet when Simon took the cross of Jesus on his own shoulders and carried it behind Jesus (Luke 23:26), he fulfilled what Jesus demanded of his disciples: "If any want to become my followers, let them deny themselves and take up their cross daily and follow me" (Luke 9:23); "Whoever does not carry the cross and follow after me cannot be my disciple" (Luke 14:27). Simon of Cyrene gives us a snapshot of discipleship: following after Jesus, carrying his cross.

What happened afterward? Did Simon drop off the cross at Calvary, walk home and forget the whole affair? There is good reason to believe otherwise. Mark describes Simon as "the father of Alexander and Rufus," as if Alexander and Rufus were Christians known by his readers. According to ancient tradition, Mark's Gospel was written in Rome. Paul, in his letter to Rome, writes, "Greet Rufus, chosen in the Lord; and greet his mother—a mother to me also" (Romans 16:13). It would seem that Simon's carrying of Jesus' cross was a turning point for him and his family.

But no matter what became of Simon afterward, his deed that day earned him a place in the Gospels and in our reflections on what it means to be a disciple of Jesus and bear our crosses as we follow him. While our crosses may be some sort of suffering that we cannot escape—a chronic illness, a difficult family situation, an irreparable harm done to us—the example of Simon throws a different light on what it means to follow after Jesus carrying a cross. It can mean shouldering the crosses of others, relieving them of their burdens and taking them on ourselves. That is what Simon did for Jesus, however involuntarily. And that is what Jesus asks us to do, voluntarily, going even the extra mile.

Paul wrote, "Bear one another's burdens, and in this way you will fulfill the law of Christ" (Galatians 6:2). Take the sufferings of others upon yourself, just as Jesus bore our infirmities (see Isaiah 53:4), just as Simon bore the cross of Jesus. Follow after Jesus, carrying not only your personal cross, whatever it may be, but also crosses of others. For in shouldering others' crosses, you, like Simon, bear the cross of Christ.

FOR REFLECTION

What is the heaviest burden I have taken on to help someone else? How have I received the strength to bear this burden?

LOW PLACES, HIGH PLACES

When you are invited by someone to a wedding banquet, do not sit down at the place of honor, in case someone more distinguished than you has been invited by your host; and the host who invited both of you may come and say to you, "Give this person your place," and then in disgrace you would start to take the lowest place. But when you are invited, go and sit down at the lowest place, so that when your host comes, he may say to you, "Friend, move up higher"; then you will be honored in the presence of all who sit at the table with you. For all who exalt themselves will be humbled, and those who humble themselves will be exalted.

LUKE 14:8–11

Someone supposedly advised that in Hollywood, "the key to success is sincerity—and if you can fake that, you have it made."

Presumably a similar cynical comment could be made about humility: "The key to honors is humility; if you pretend to be humble, you will get the honors you crave."

But is that what Jesus is trying to teach us? Did he tell us that it is in our self-interest to take a lower place at table so that we might be honored with a higher place? Is he proposing a show of humbleness as the shrewdest route to being exalted?

We know this cannot be Jesus' meaning. True humility does not set its sights on honors; it is sham humility to humble oneself only in order to be exalted. Yet paradoxically, the humble person will be honored by God—honored for not lusting after honors. God is smart enough to sort out genuine humility from a self-seeking show of sham humility and to reward the one who is not looking for rewards.

Jesus has more than this in mind, however, as indicated by similar teachings on other occasions. "The greatest among you will be your servant. All who exalt themselves will be humbled, and all who humble themselves will be exalted" (Matthew 23:11–12). Again, "The greatest among you must become like the youngest, and the leader like the one who serves…. I am among you as one who serves" (Luke 22:26–27).

True greatness does not mean sitting at the head of the table, being waited on and honored. True greatness is found at the foot of the table, waiting on others. That is where Jesus is, gird in a towel, washing our dirty feet. "If I, your Lord and Teacher, have washed your feet, you also ought to wash one another's feet. For I set you an example, that you also should do as I have done to you" (John 13:14–15).

Those who renounce honors and choose humble service do so in imitation of Christ, who "came not to be served but to serve, and to give his life [as] a ransom for many" (Mark 10:45). Paul urged his readers to make the attitude of Christ their own, he who "did not regard equality with God as something to be exploited, but emptied himself, taking the form of a slave" (Philippians 2:6–7). He "humbled himself," demonstrating the meaning of true humility, and "became obedient to the point of death—even death on a cross" (Philippians 2:8).

Paul continues, "Therefore God also highly exalted him" (Philippians 2:9). Jesus is the preeminent example of the one who humbles himself and then is exalted. He is now exalted over all creation, so that "at the name of Jesus every knee should bend, in heaven and on earth and under the earth" (Philippians 2:10). Where he is we hope to be, joined with him and sharing in his glory. Jesus is the ultimate model, not only for lowly service but also for its reward.

Those who choose the lower places, those who choose a life of service, will be lifted up by God, raised to heavenly life, where God will handle the seating arrangements in his eternal banquet.

FOR REFLECTION

How have I already experienced Jesus lifting me up when I lowered myself to serve? Am I in any relationships or situations in which I need to be less concerned about myself and more concerned about someone else?

HOW TALENTED ARE YOU?

For it is as if a man, going on a journey, summoned his slaves and entrusted his property; to one he gave five talents, to another two, to another one, to each according to his ability.

MATTHEW 25:14–15

Are you a one-talent person, a three-talent person or a five-talent person?

And what's a talent anyway?

In very ancient times a talent was a unit of weight, roughly forty-five pounds. By New Testament times the word had come to connote that weight of gold or silver and therefore was a measure of wealth. It has this meaning in the parable of the talents: Three men are given various sizable sums of money to invest during their master's absence.

Writers in the Middle Ages, with Jesus' parable of the talents in mind, began to use the word *talent* as a poetic expression for endowments and abilities that one had been given. Their figurative use eventually became the common meaning of the word. The origins of this meaning in Jesus' parable still linger, for our notion of talent is related to the idea of gift: To say, "She is a gifted pianist," means much the same as to say, "She is a talented pianist."

The point of Jesus' parable is not simply that we ought to use our God-given gifts and abilities to their fullest. The context in which Jesus told this parable makes it clear that he had a more specific message in mind. Chapters 24 and 25 of Matthew's Gospel are a unified block of teaching, devoted to the end of this age (see Matthew 24:3). Jesus addressed the question of when it would happen, but for the most part he spoke about what we should do while awaiting his return.

Jesus held up the example of a "faithful and wise servant, whom his master has put in charge of his household, to give the other slaves their allowance of food at the proper time" (Matthew 24:45). The disciples of Jesus were likewise to be faithful in carrying out the responsibilities he had given them, until he returned. Jesus might not return as soon as they expected, and they had to be prudently prepared for this possibility—the point of the parable of the ten bridesmaids (Matthew 25:1–13).

What are the responsibilities Jesus gave to his disciples? Jesus concluded his discourse with a Last Judgment scene. Then he would say to his faithful and prudent servants, "I was hungry and you gave me food, I was thirsty and you gave me something to drink" (Matthew 25:35). Caring for those in need is a high-priority responsibility for Jesus' followers as they await his return, for in caring for them they care for him.

This is the context in which Jesus told the parable of the talents. Every follower of Jesus has been given certain abilities, gifts, resources, charisms, skills, aptitudes; our talents come in a wide variety of colors and sizes. Some of us may be more gifted than others; there may be one-talent disciples and three-talent disciples and five-talent disciples. But no disciple of Jesus is completely ungifted. Every follower of Jesus is equipped in one way or another to be a "faithful and wise servant" who distributes food to the hungry, solace to the mourning or justice to the wronged. Every one of us is equipped in some way to be commended by Jesus at the Last Judgment for having served him in the least of his brothers and sisters.

The questions each of us must ask ourselves are, therefore, "What are my talents?" "How have I been equipped and gifted to serve Jesus?" "What are the one, three or five abilities with which I have been entrusted to use in the service of others?" "How well am I using them?" It might not be a bad idea to make a list of your talents and periodically review how you are using them as an examination of conscience.

It doesn't matter whether we have one talent or five talents: The number of talents we have been given is God's responsibility, not ours. Nor does it matter all that much whether our talents equip us to do mighty works or only modest deeds: That, too, is in God's hands. What does matter is what we do with what we have been given. That matters eternally—as Jesus' description of the Last Judgment makes clear.

FOR REFLECTION

What are my chief skills, talents, gifts? What do I do best? What do I most enjoy doing? How am I using my abilities to serve Jesus?

RESOURCES

The land of a rich man produced abundantly. And he thought to himself, "What should I do, for I have no place to store my crops?" Then he said, "I will do this: I will pull down my barns and build larger ones, and there I will store all my grain and my goods. And I will say to my soul, 'Soul, you have ample goods laid up for many years; relax, eat, drink, be merry.'" But God said to him, "You fool! This very night your life is being demanded of you. And the things you have prepared, whose will they be?" So it is with those who store up treasures for themselves but are not rich toward God.

LUKE 12:16–21

What was the rich man to do? His barns weren't big enough to hold his harvest, so he built bigger barns. Should we condemn a farmer who does the same today? It would be irresponsible for a farmer not to store his harvest, leaving it exposed to the weather.

The fault of the rich man in the parable does not lie in what he did but in what he did not do, and in his attitudes. He considered his resources to be his own, to do with as he liked. He thought that his resources would assure a safe and comfortable life. He intended to use them solely for his own pleasure.

Jesus' parable points out the illusion of believing that wealth can provide security and happiness. No matter how big our barns or how thick the bank vault and how much money we have in it, wealth cannot make us secure. Rich or poor, our lives are in the hands of God. For someone who wants to be completely independent, this may be a disappointment. But for someone who is willing to trust God, this can be a great relief.

Our Father in heaven knows our needs; there is no reason for us to be anxious (Matthew 6:31–32). Jesus said that it is the "Gentiles," which in context means those who are not God's people, who strive for what they will eat and drink (Matthew 6:32). This does not mean that God's people will end up having less to eat than those who are not or that we will not have to work at jobs as others have to or that we should have smaller barns than others. It means that we should never look to money or large, well-filled barns for the security that only our Father can give.

The rich man of the parable did not intend to use his resources to benefit anyone but himself—the opposite of what Jesus taught we are to do with our resources. Jesus told his disciples, "Sell your possessions, and give alms. Make purses for yourselves that do not wear out, an unfailing treasure in heaven, where no thief comes near and no moth destroys" (Luke 12:33). Jesus invited a rich man to sell what he had and to give the proceeds to the poor (Luke 18:22), and he commended Zacchaeus for giving half of his possessions to the poor (Luke 19:8–10). Jesus told a parable about a Samaritan who helped someone in need; then he said, "Go and do likewise" (Luke 10:37).

In contrast to these teachings, the rich man of this parable only thought of himself and his own pleasure. Perhaps he would have been commended by Jesus if he had said to himself, "This is what I will do: I will modestly enlarge my barns to help hold this bountiful harvest, but I will give away to the poor what is beyond my needs. I will say to myself, 'Rejoice in God, who has been so generous in his blessing.' And now that I do not need to work so hard, I will spend more time with my wife and children."

Our first step in learning how God wants us to use our resources is to acknowledge that this is indeed something that we need to find out. We cannot separate our possessions and our financial goals from our following of Jesus.

FOR REFLECTION

How generous am I toward those in need? What would I need to do in order to free up money so that I could give it away?

ABIDING IN JESUS

Abide in me as I abide in you. Just as the branch cannot bear fruit by itself unless it abides in the vine, neither can you unless you abide in me. I am the vine, you are the branches. Those who abide in me and I in them bear much fruit, because apart from me you can do nothing.... As the Father has loved me, so I have loved you; abide in my love. If you keep my commandments, you will abide in my love, just as I have kept my Father's commandments and abide in his love.

JOHN 15:4–5, 9–10

One very significant word in John's Gospel is the word *abide*—sometimes translated as "stay" or "remain" or "dwell." It can have a very ordinary meaning, as it does when two disciples first met Jesus and asked him, "'Where are you *staying*?' He said to them, 'Come and see.' They came and saw where he was *staying*, and they *remained* with him that day" (John 1:38–39; italics added).

But this ordinary meaning opens up to a more profound meaning: for these two disciples to remain (or abide) with Jesus that day was the beginning of their remaining with him forever, abiding in him as the source of eternal life.

Abiding with Jesus draws us into the relationship Jesus has with his Father. Jesus proclaimed, "I am in the Father and the Father is in me" (John 14:11); the works Jesus did were the works of "the Father who dwells [abides] in me" (John 14:10). Jesus prayed that his disciples would enter into his relationship with his Father: "As you, Father, are in me and I am in you, may they also be in us" (John 17:21). The intimate union of the Father and the Son was extended through the Son to his disciples.

In its richest meaning, therefore, to abide in Jesus means to be permanently and intimately united with him, sharing in his intimate union with his Father. This is not a fringe benefit that comes with being a Christian; this is what it means to be a Christian.

Jesus had a way of expressing profound truths in simple language, and he chose a grapevine as an image for what it means to abide in him. His first listeners were very familiar with grapevines, which are common in Palestine. Every branch of a grapevine draws its life from the vine and is able to bear grapes because it is part of the vine. A branch that is cut off from the vine bears no fruit; it withers and dies.

So too, Jesus taught, apart from him we are fruitless and dead. But united with him we share his life, just as a branch shares the life of the vine. The life we share with Jesus is the life he shares with his Father. If we abide in Jesus, we abide in his love. This requires that we keep the commandments he has given us (John 15:10)—just as Jesus did his Father's will, so must we, if we are to remain in union with them.

Yet it should be clear that abiding in Jesus involves more than obeying commandments. We can obey rules and laws impersonally, but Jesus is inviting us to a lot more. He is inviting us to enter into an intimate relationship with him and his Father. He is offering to have their life flow through us, as the life of a grapevine flows into its branches. He is promising to make our lives fruitful. He is promising that our relationship with him and his Father will never end, for the life that they give us is eternal life.

Jesus expressed all this with a very simple but profound invitation: "Abide in me as I abide in you" (John 15:4)—abide in me forever; come and see where I dwell, and remain with me forever.

FOR REFLECTION

How is Jesus drawing me to him? What response do I need to make to him?

SEVEN

THE WAY TO
RESURRECTION

You have the words of eternal life.

JOHN 6:68

REMEMBER ME

*When they came to the place that is called The
Skull, they crucified Jesus there with the criminals, one on his right and one on his left....*

*One of the criminals who were hanged
there kept deriding him and saying, "Are you
not the Messiah? Save yourself and us!" But
the other rebuked him, saying, "Do you not
fear God, since you are under the same sentence of condemnation? And we indeed have
been condemned justly, for we are getting what
we deserve for our deeds, but this man has
done nothing wrong." Then he said, "Jesus,
remember me when you come into your kingdom." He replied, "Truly I tell you, today you
will be with me in Paradise."*

LUKE 23:33, 39–43

Crucifixion was death by public torture, a slow and horrible form of execution. It was a sentence usually reserved for violent criminals, insurrectionists and slaves. We are not told what the two men executed with Jesus had done, but by the admission of one of them, it was serious enough to merit this agonizing death.

We should therefore not romanticize the "good thief," imagining him to be a noble person who happened to steal for a living—a "robber with a heart of gold." It is better to take him at his word: He had committed crimes deserving of the worst punishment.

Yet even this criminal could recognize that Jesus' death was a setup. The inscription over Jesus' head read, "This is the King of the Jews" (Luke 23:38). This was the legal charge against Jesus: He was executed as a rebel against Roman rule—a patently false charge (see Luke 23:2–5, 14–15).

The inscription was put up to mock Jesus. It was one more taunt in a crescendo of mockery on Calvary that day. "If you are King of the Jews, save yourself!" was the jeer of the religious leaders, the Roman soldiers and one of the criminals being executed with Jesus (Luke 23:35–39).

The other criminal refused to join in this mockery. Even though he had committed serious crimes, he could tell the difference between deserved and undeserved punishment. Jesus did not deserve to be crucified and jeered at, and this criminal said so.

He also said, "Jesus, remember me when you come into your kingdom."

This criminal did not address Jesus with the title "Lord," as a follower of Jesus might have done, so we should not read too full an act of faith into his words. How much did he know or understand of Jesus' kingdom? Unless he was given some direct revelation by God, it was probably not much; even those who had followed Jesus throughout his public ministry did not really understand the nature of his kingdom (see Acts 1:6).

In essence, what this criminal did was "unmock" Jesus. He acknowledged the truth that everyone else was conspiring to obscure with their jeers: Jesus was being unjustly put to death. He took the taunts being heaped on Jesus and turned them into a respectful request. Where others mocked Jesus by calling him a Messiah-king, this criminal spoke to him as if he really were a king and would have power to dispense favors. "Remember me, criminal though I am, when you begin your reign."

Jesus in response said that he would indeed remember this criminal and that they would be together that day in Paradise. This man who deserved the wretched death of crucifixion became, in a sense, the first canonized saint, the only saint canonized by Jesus himself. What a glorious reward for a few respectful words—uttered by one who had committed serious sins and may not have understood all that much about Jesus.

The cross is an index of God's love for us, an index of the lengths to which he will go to forgive us. Jesus' canonization of a criminal who died beside him is an indication of what he wants to do for everyone. We can certainly make at least as much response to Jesus as did this criminal and hope for as great a reward.

FOR REFLECTION

What hope does Jesus give me in his promise that the criminal would be with him in paradise?

ARISE!

Some people came from the leader's house to say, "Your daughter is dead. Why trouble the teacher any further?" But overhearing what they said, Jesus said to the leader of the synagogue, "Do not fear, only believe." ...He took her by the hand and said to her, "Talitha cum," which means, "Little girl, get up!" And immediately the girl got up and began to walk about.

MARK 5:35–36, 41–42

At Easter we celebrate the resurrection of Jesus Christ as well as our own hope of rising with him. If Jesus had not been raised from the dead, our faith would be in vain, and we would have no hope of resurrection (1 Corinthians 15:12–18). But since Christ is risen, we who are joined with him look forward to being united with him in resurrection (Romans 6:5).

Seen in the light of Easter, Jesus' raising of the daughter of the synagogue leader Jairus prefigures our own resurrection. The girl was dead, and her neighbors in Capernaum were mourning her, but Jesus said, "Why do you make a commotion and weep? The child is not dead but sleeping" (Mark 5:39). Jesus was not denying the reality of her death but saying that her death, like sleep, would come to an end. He would wake her from death by a word, just as one calls upon someone who is sleeping to arise.

The word Jesus used was *cum*, the ordinary Aramaic word for "get up" or "arise." Mark translated Jesus' Aramaic words into Greek for the benefit of readers who did not know Aramaic: Jesus "said to her, 'Talitha cum,' which means, 'Little girl, get up!'"

Mark's translation would have been a signal to his readers that there was a deeper meaning in this event than the restoration of life to this girl. The Greek verb that Mark used to translate Jesus' command of "get up!" or "arise!" is the same Greek verb that is used in the New Testament for Jesus' own Resurrection. Jesus was raised from the dead; Jesus raised this girl from the dead—and Jesus will raise us from the dead.

Jairus was not the only official in Capernaum to seek the help of Jesus in the face of death. A Roman centurion stationed in Capernaum had a servant who was "ill and close to death" (Luke 7:2). When Jesus said he would come and cure him, the centurion replied, "Lord, do not trouble yourself, for I am not worthy to have you come under my roof; therefore I did not presume to come to you. But only speak the word, and let my servant be healed" (Luke 7:6–7).

Our prayer at Mass before Communion echoes the centurion: "Lord, I am not worthy to receive you, but only say the word and I shall be healed." One day while reciting this prayer, the question occurred to me: Just what is the word that I am imploring Jesus to say in order that I be healed? The parallel between the two officials from Capernaum came to mind, and I realized that in echoing the centurion's request I was really asking for the word that Jesus spoke to the synagogue official's daughter. The word I need Jesus to say to me is "arise!"

"Only say the word, and I shall be healed." Ultimately the healing we need from Jesus is not from arthritis or heart disease, or from this or that sin, but the full healing of resurrection. We need and welcome his partial healings along the way to resurrection, but they are only partial. He may heal us of our ailments, but the way of all flesh nevertheless leads to death. He forgives our sins, but we find ourselves committing them again or finding new ones to commit. We will always stand in need of physical and spiritual healing until we are granted the ultimate and final healing of resurrection, freeing us forever from sin and pain.

We therefore pray to the Risen Jesus: Speak your word to me; command me to arise. Raise me up now from my sins and illnesses. Raise me up on the last day to eternal life. Say only the word "Arise!" and I shall truly be healed.

FOR REFLECTION

Where am I most in need of healing? What word do I most wish Jesus would speak to me?

LISTEN TO HIM!

Six days later, Jesus took with him Peter and James and John, and led them up a high mountain apart, by themselves. And he was transfigured before them, and his clothes became dazzling white, such as no one on earth could bleach them…. Then a cloud over-shadowed them, and from the cloud there came a voice, "This is my Son, the Beloved; listen to him!"

MARK 9:2–3, 7

If we compare Mark's accounts of Jesus' Baptism and of his Transfiguration, we find both similarities and differences.

The Father spoke from heaven on both occasions—the only times that we hear the Father speaking in Mark's Gospel. On both occasions the Father stated that Jesus was his Son, his beloved (Mark 1:11; 9:7).

But whereas the Father spoke to Jesus at the time of his Baptism, during the Transfiguration he spoke to Peter and James and John: "This is my Son, the Beloved." And at the

Transfiguration the Father added an admonition, again clearly addressed to the three disciples: "Listen to him!"

This command to listen to Jesus was not merely a command for Peter, James and John but a command for all who would follow Jesus. We know we should listen to whatever Jesus says to us. But the context of the passage in Mark's Gospel suggests that the Father's command has a specific application. The Father was saying, "Pay particular attention to what Jesus has just taught you and will teach you after you go down from the mountain."

Jesus' Transfiguration occurred right after his first foretelling of his coming passion and death (Mark 8:31) and shortly before his second warning of how he would die (Mark 9:31). In each case the disciples failed to understand what Jesus was talking about (Mark 8:32; 9:32). They could not conceive that the Messiah would suffer and die; they were hoping to reap personal rewards by following a triumphant messiah (see Mark 10:37, 41).

Let us consider in more detail the flow of words and events in Mark: Peter acknowledged Jesus as the Messiah (Mark 8:29); Jesus immediately told of his coming rejection, suffering, death and rising (Mark 8:31); Peter refused to accept this (Mark 8:32); Jesus rebuked Peter for rejecting God's way (Mark 8:33); Jesus taught that anyone who wants to follow him must lay down his life and accept the same fate as he himself would suffer (Mark 8:34–36).

Jesus was then transfigured (Mark 9:2–8), and he referred again to his suffering (Mark 9:12). After expelling a demon that the disciples could not (Mark 9:14–29), Jesus again spoke of his death (Mark 9:31), but his followers did not understand what he was talking about (Mark 9:32). They argued among themselves over who was greatest (Mark 9:33–34), an argument Jesus resolved by teaching that anyone who wants to be great must be last and servant of all (Mark 9:35)—which is to say, must imitate his own example of self-sacrificing service.

It is in the midst of this that the Father said, "Listen to him!" From the context we can understand the Father to be saying, "Listen to my Son when he speaks of his mission to serve and when he calls you to serve. Listen to him when he speaks of laying down his own life and when he invites you to lay down your lives in imitation of him.

"Listen to him when he teaches that the path of earthly power and honor is not the path that he will follow as the Messiah and not the path that his followers are to take either. Listen to him when he speaks of his cross and invites you to take up your crosses and follow in his footsteps. Listen to him when he reveals the great mystery that those who lose their lives for his sake will save them.

"Do not be slow to understand; do not be concerned about yourselves; do not reject the cross. Rather, listen to my beloved Son, and follow the path he is taking. It is the path that leads to life for him and for you."

FOR REFLECTION

Do I take the words of Jesus in the Gospels as his words to me? How diligent am I in letting his words shape my life?

LIFE FROM DEATH

Jesus began to weep. So the Jews said, "See how he loved him!"… Then Jesus, again greatly disturbed, came to the tomb. It was a cave, and a stone was lying against it. Jesus said, "Take

away the stone." Martha, the sister of the dead
man, said to him, "Lord, already there is a
stench because he has been dead four days."
Jesus said to her, "Did I not tell you that if you
believed, you would see the glory of God?" So
they took away the stone. And Jesus looked
upward and said, "Father, I thank you for hav-
ing heard me." ...When he had said this, he
cried with a loud voice, "Lazarus, come out!"

JOHN 11:35–36, 38–41, 43

The Gospels present us with three people whom Jesus raised from the dead: the daughter of Jairus (Mark 5:21–24, 35–43), the son of the widow of Nain (Luke 7:11–16) and Lazarus of Bethany, brother of Mary and Martha (John 11:1–44). Since our ultimate hope in Jesus is that he will also raise us from our graves, it is worth reflecting on what these incidents teach us.

One noteworthy feature of these three incidents is the compassion of Jesus. He went to Jairus's house in response to his plea on behalf of his daughter (Mark 5:22–24). He didn't wait to be asked to do something for the only son of the widow of Nain: When Jesus saw her, "he had compassion for her and said to her, 'Do not weep' " (Luke 7:13). Mary and Martha sent a message to Jesus, "Lord, he who you love is ill" (John 11:3). His love for Lazarus was obvious to everyone who saw him at the tomb.

If we were to ask what Lazarus and the daughter of Jairus and the son of the widow did to deserve being raised from the dead, we would be hard pressed to come up with much. There is no indication that Jesus ever met Jairus's daughter before he restored her to life; he simply responded to her father's request. Likewise, there is no indication that he had previously known the mother and son of Nain; Jesus, rather, acted out of spontaneous compassion. Lazarus and his sisters were close friends of Jesus: He ate with them (John 12:1–3) and probably stayed in their home in Bethany on the Mount of Olives when he was in Jerusalem (Matthew 21:17). Yet again the Gospels say nothing to indicate that Lazarus particularly deserved what must be regarded as the greatest of miracles, to be brought back to life after having died.

That very fact holds out great hope for us. What we look forward to in Christ Jesus—resurrection to eternal life—is something humanly impossible to achieve. It is beyond the capability of medical science to restore life to someone who is corrupting in the tomb. How much more impossible it is for us to give ourselves unending life in glorified bodies! Nor is this something we can earn. Even if we behave very well in this life, even if we obey God's laws perfectly, eternal life is not something we are capable of earning as our due.

By clumsy analogy we might imagine ourselves owning a particularly nice canary: No matter how beautifully it sang, it could never earn the right to be transformed so that it would live for a hundred thousand years. So, too, we can never earn what we hope to receive: resurrection in Christ Jesus to eternal life. It is something that we will be given, not that we will merit, no matter how good we are.

This truth is symbolized in the three Gospel incidents we have been examining. In every case Jesus raised the dead person out of compassion; in no case was it something that the dead person earned or was due. The most the dead person could have done was to have been a friend of Jesus during his or her lifetime and asked to receive new life from him or had others ask on his or her behalf.

Life from death is something that Jesus freely gives us—but also eagerly gives, because he is the compassion of God come among us. God gives us life because he loves us.

What are the implications for me of Jesus' raising of Lazarus, the daughter of Jairus and the widow's son? What does it mean for me that Jesus loved Lazarus and was moved with compassion for a widow?

THE SEED OF LIFE

Jesus answered them, "The hour has come for the Son of Man to be glorified. Very truly, I tell you, unless a grain of wheat falls into the earth and dies, it remains just a single grain; but if it dies, it bears much fruit. Those who love their life lose it, and those who hate their life in this world will keep it for eternal life. Whoever serves me must follow me, and where I am, there will my servant be also. Whoever serves me, the Father will honor."

JOHN 12:23–26

To our normal human way of thinking, death is the ultimate evil, the ultimate tragedy, the ultimate negation. Yet Jesus called his coming death his hour of glorification! This is a jolting reversal of human logic—akin to calling a severe famine a blessing or leprosy an honor. To be executed on a cross is glorification? How can this be?

Jesus used an analogy to help us accept the logic of the cross. When a seed is planted, it is as if it has died and been buried. But a plant springs forth from this "dying," and when the seed is no more, the plant has taken its place. The plant is not the seed but new life that has sprung forth from the seed. Should a seed refuse to be sown in the ground, it would remain a seed and eventually rot or dry up and lose its life. It is only in accepting the death of being sown that a seed is able to produce new and transformed life.

Jesus' eye was on the transformed life that he would have through dying, and therefore he could rightly call his dying his glorification. Jesus invites us to have the same faith and to follow him along the same path of life through death. To be a disciple of Jesus is ultimately a matter of letting him take us by the hand and lead us along the way of the cross, for that is the path to eternal life.

It is not an easy path, for it is a path of faith rather than sight. New life springs forth only after a seed has been sown; the seed cannot see the plant it will become. So too in this life we cannot see the new life that Jesus promises us. Our eyes can only see as far as our being sown in death; they cannot see the final stage of our journey with Jesus, when we will be joined with him in the presence of his Father. We must follow after Jesus in faith.

Such faith is not always easy to sustain. Some of Saint Paul's converts in Corinth doubted whether they would rise from the dead, a doubt that threatened the core of the gospel message. Paul addressed this doubt in the fifteenth chapter of his first letter to Corinth: "If there is no resurrection of the dead, then Christ has not been raised; and if Christ has not been raised, then our proclamation has been in vain and your faith has been in vain.... If for this life only we have hoped in Christ, we are of all people most to be pitied" (1 Corinthians 15:13–14, 19).

Paul made use of the same seed-and-plant analogy as did Jesus in order to help his Corinthian converts embrace the mystery of life through death:

What you sow does not come to life unless it dies. And as for what you sow, you do not sow the body that is to be, but a bare seed, perhaps of wheat or of some other grain. But God gives it a body as he has chosen, and to each kind of seed its own body…. So it is with the resurrection of the dead. What is sown is perishable, what is raised imperishable. (1 Corinthians 15:36–38, 42)

Our faith that we will follow Jesus through death to glorification should shape how we live this life. We do not need to waste our energies in a futile attempt to cling to this life and the things of this life as if they are all we have. We are free to devote ourselves totally to following and serving Jesus. We are free to live in the present, because we do not need to be anxious about the eternal future. We can follow after Jesus even along the way of the cross, because we know where the path ends.

The great mystery of our faith is of life through death: the death and resurrection of Jesus Christ and our participation in his conquest of death.

FOR REFLECTION

Am I able to look upon death as a doorway? What do my faith and hope tell me is on the other side of the door?

BEING WITH JESUS

Simon Peter said to him, "Lord, where are you going?" Jesus answered, "Where I am going, you cannot follow me now; but you will follow me afterward….

"In my Father's house there are many dwelling places. If it were not so, would I have told you that I go to prepare a place for you? And if I go and prepare a place for you, I will

*come again and will take you to myself, so that
where I am, there you may be also."*

JOHN 13:36; 14:2–3

During the Last Supper "Jesus knew that his hour had come to depart from this world and go to the Father. Having loved his own who were in the world, he loved them to the end" (John 13:1). Jesus shared a final meal with the disciples, and in the course of it he spoke of his departure. "I came from the Father and have come into the world; again, I am leaving the world and am going to the Father" (John 16:28).

The disciples were grief stricken at the prospect of Jesus' departure (John 16:6). But Jesus told them, "Do not let your hearts be troubled" (John 14:27). He gave them two reassurances. First, he promised the coming of the Holy Spirit: "It is to your advantage that I go away, for if I do not go away, the Advocate will not come to you" (John 16:7). The Spirit would be the continuing presence of Jesus to his followers during their lives on earth.

Jesus gave his followers another reassurance: Although he was departing, the separation would be only temporary. He told them that he was going ahead of his disciples to prepare a place for them; he promised that he would "take you to myself, so that where I am, there you may be also."

John's Gospel is filled with the invitation to and promise of eternal life; indeed, that is why John wrote his Gospel (John 20:31). Yet we are given very little description of what eternal life will be like. While we are promised that we will not be thirsty or hungry (John 4:13–14; 6:35), our questions about the nature of life after death are largely left unanswered. Yet we are told one very important fact: Eternal life means being with Jesus. John's Gospel presents us with an invitation to eternal life and the assurance that this means being with Jesus in a place he has prepared for us, which means being with his Father, and it invites us to cling to these hopes.

The First Letter of John goes a step farther. It proclaims that in eternity, we will not only be with God but be like him. "Beloved, we are God's children now; what we will be has not yet been revealed. What we do know is this: when he is revealed, we will be like him, for we shall see him as he is" (1 John 3:2). We cannot now see the Risen Jesus with bodily eyes, nor can we see the Father: "No one has ever seen God" (John 1:18). But in being raised to be with Jesus, we will also be transformed to be like him, able to see him as he is, able to be with him and his Father for eternity.

Jesus' death on Calvary was his going on ahead of us to his Father. Our hope as his disciples is that our deaths will be our going to Jesus, going to the place he has prepared for us, coming into the presence of his Father. As Jesus was raised, so too we will be raised—not brought back to this life as was Lazarus but given new life, eternal life. We will be with Jesus and see him; we will be transformed to be like him. Our hope should give us great joy, as we anticipate what lies ahead for us.

FOR REFLECTION

Am I consciously trying to live in union with Jesus now, in preparation for abiding with him forever? How might I grow closer to him?

NOTES

CHAPTER ONE: GETTING TO KNOW JESUS

1. Walter Abbott, trans., *Documents of Vatican II* (Piscataway, N.J.: New Century, 1966), p. 119.

CHAPTER TWO: PONDERING HIS LOVE

1. Hans Walter Wolff, *Hosea (Hermeneia: A Historical and Critical Commentary)*, trans. Gary Stansell (Minneapolis: Fortress, 1974), p. 105.

CHAPTER THREE: THE FRIENDS OF JESUS

1. John Wilkinson, *Egeria's Travels to the Holy Land* (Warminster, England: Aris & Phillips, 1981), p. 194.

CHAPTER FIVE: TO PRAY AS JESUS

1. Kenneth E. Bailey, *Poet and Peasant* (Grand Rapids, Mich.: Eerdmans, 1976), pp. 119–133.

INDEX OF INITIAL
SCRIPTURE PASSAGES

LUKE

JOHN